Silhouette Style

Nanetta Bananto

Silhouette
Style

Techniques and Template Sets for Papercut Projects

Nanetta Bananto

NORTH LIGHT BOOKS
Cincinnati, Ohio

Published by North Light Books, an imprint of F+W Media, Inc., 4700 East Galbraith Road, Cincinnati, Ohio, 45236. (800) 289-0963. First Edition.

14 13 12 11 10   5 4 3 2 1

DISTRIBUTED IN CANADA BY FRASER DIRECT
100 Armstrong Avenue
Georgetown, ON, Canada L7G 5S4
Tel: (905) 877-4411

DISTRIBUTED IN THE U.K. AND EUROPE BY DAVID & CHARLES
Brunel House, Newton Abbot, Devon, TQ12 4PU, England
Tel: (+44) 1626 323200, Fax: (+44) 1626 323319
E-mail: postmaster@davidandcharles.co.uk

DISTRIBUTED IN AUSTRALIA BY CAPRICORN LINK
P.O. Box 704, S. Windsor NSW, 2756 Australia
Tel: (02) 4577-3555

Library of Congress Cataloging in Publication Data
Bananto, Nanetta, 1959-
  Silhouette style : techniques and template sets for papercut projects / Nanetta Bananto.
    p. cm.
  Includes index.
  ISBN-13: 978-1-4403-0318-0 (pbk. : alk. paper)
  ISBN-10: 1-4403-0318-5 (alk. paper)
  1. Paper work. 2. Silhouettes. I. Title.
  TT870.B234 2010
  745.592--dc22
              2010020735

www.fwmedia.com.

Edited by Liz Casler
Designed by Corrie Schaffeld
Production coordinated by Greg Nock
Photography by Christine Polomsky, Al Parrish

About the Author

Nanetta is an artist and author creating original artworks in the heart of Kansas. Her days are filled with design, color and possibility. Although her head is full of fanciful images, it was with a self-taught resolution that she learned to engineer organic curves and minute details, translating them into a digital form.

Paper has always been a part of Nanetta's expression. She has designed numerous CD covers and posters for independent artists and events as well as illustrated children's menus.

Polymer clay, the medium of her first book with North Light, became a favorite when she discovered it in the early 1980s. She has authored many tutorials for Polyform Products, given workshops and produced countless works, including dolls, jewelry, sculpture, corporate displays and fairies from this versatile medium. Nanetta is also now experimenting with bronze and copper clays.

The paper designs in this book are just the beginning of Nanetta's digital works. She continues to add to her own collection of files, adding shoe patterns, chairs and trees that stand on their own. Nanetta's art continues to evolve and explore the melding of old world craft and new millennia technology.

Metric Conversion Chart

To convert	to	multiply by
Inches	Centimeters	2.54
Centimeters	Inches	0.4
Feet	Centimeters	30.5
Centimeters	Feet	0.03
Yards	Meters	0.9
Meters	Yards	1.1

Dedication

I dedicate this book to my husband, Mark Horton, who is my everything and a kite.

And to Nick Bananto, Natalie Blanco, Jasmine, Winnie, TJ, Isaiah and Matt, Charlie and Walt Hein, Tony Bananto, Bruce Bananto, W.S. Bananto, Tom and Stacey Hora, Niall Horton, Elliot Horton, Marcia Horton, Rich Horton, Rev. Dwight and Louise Horton, Jay Antol.

Acknowledgments

Special thanks for your continued support and spirit:

Trish, Scott, Homer, Gail, Greg, CeCe, Dona, Michael, Marilyn, Carol, Mary, Claudette, Martha, Rita, Jim, Linda, Lana, Dick, Elaine, Lisa, Hannah, Ella, Leah, Betty, Barbara, Liv, Margery, Kam, Dave, Hugh, Jack, Valerie, Mike, Johanna, Preston, Tammy, Shannon, Jess, Nikki, Gary, Deb, Rosalee, Dulcie, Karen, Brian, Bryan, Juli, Barney, Shalen, Mark, Emily, Andy, Kelly, Ron, Jill, Pam, Pat, Marsha, Joann, Lincoln, Lissa, Sig, Bill, Josh, Dee, Kurt, Cindy, Stephanie, Cheryl, Marge, Chris, Phil, Laurie, Guinn, Lynn, Theresa, Marta, Tanya, Wayne, Sunny, Sierra, Marshall, Leslie, Jet, Jette, Joni, Joanie, Tim, Deborah, Craig, Kent, Cassi, Dennis, Christa, Jackie, Sarah, Nancy, Jan, Chad, Peggy, David, Annie, Julie, Kathleen, Tonia, Pamela, Mo, Fernando, Charolette, Charlotte, Jessica, Billy, Maureen, Ned, Lynne, Sheryl, Susan, Becky, Ellie, Sandy, Bryce, Chuck and Ernest Tubb.

Thank you for sponsoring me through the writing of this book:

Accugraphic, for sending me the KNK Maxx to cut all the projects perfectly.
Sasnak, Carlos O'Kelly's Mexican Café
Carol Hill and Mary Jabara
Bruce T. Bananto, Inc.
Jim Keefer, for the pile of polished paper.

And a prayer for those who have gone on whose art touched my life:

Joe Bananto, K.C. Haywood, Janet Mullen, Kelly Slack, Kirk Rundstrom, Lester Raymer, Malcolm Esping, Dr. Geraldine Hammond, Bill Hulvey

Table of Contents

Introduction

The silhouette has been a common element in art for centuries. We can find silhouettes all around us, be it in the shadow of a tree branch on a sidewalk or a deer against a sunset. Silhouettes are perhaps most well known from portraiture. Eighteenth-century artists cut silhouette portraits freehand from paper, while amateur enthusiasts traced the shadows of loved ones onto black paper, then cut them out and framed them. These were kept much as we now keep photos to remember a family member.

After photography was widely available, the silhouette fell out of favor for portraiture but continued to be found in architecture, illustration, textile design, metalwork, and more right up until the present. Today's silhouette is fresh and new with classic styles in contemporary colors.

You can use the silhouettes in this book by themselves—plain and simple—or embellish them, incorporating other media such as pencil, ink, marker or whatever else your paper will accommodate.

Included in the back of the book are thumbnails of all the designs. You'll also find a CD containing digital files of all the silhouettes used in the projects within these pages, plus bonus designs to expand artistic possibilities. The designs are made to interchange with one another. Mix and match these designs for endless combinations. The seaweed graphic file works as well in a marine setting as it does in a forest. Turn it upside down to trim a fairy dress. Let these designs open your imagination.

Since the design files are in .eps format, they can be imported into your software program such as Adobe Photoshop or CorelDRAW. You may need to convert the .eps file to the correct format for your cutting machine. Though this book represents what can be done with paper, consider that this universal format can be used not only in electronic cutters, but other digital machines as well. The silhouettes are appropriate for fabric appliqué, woodcraft, embroidery, shrink plastic and more. If you decide to cut the designs by hand, import the PDF files into your image editing software and print them from your computer.

CHAPTER ONE

Materials and Techniques

The finished look of your project depends on the quality of your materials and tools. This doesn't always mean buying the most expensive brands, but many items are cheap for a reason. Tools should work easily and comfortably and often the cheapest versions don't. Avoid novelties like mini kits. Papers are so trendy that you can get beautiful papers on sale often. Paper packs and stacks are a great value and ripe with variety. I have grown to love papers I thought I'd never use when I bought them included with others I liked.

The projects in this book are designed with a personal electronic cutter in mind, but the designs can be created by hand as well. The techniques for hand cutting I've outlined in this section, such as using a pounce wheel to make fold lines, are the fruit of years of creating paper art myself by hand. The techniques that follow are not difficult, but many require careful attention and the most important tool of all: patience. Approach these projects as entertainment and it will be easy to enjoy the time it takes to make something by hand. Patience always shows.

Materials and Tools

PAPERS

Cardstock

Crisp cardstock works best for silhouette cutting. Some bargain cardstock can be too soft and can tear easily, resulting in inferior cuts. Expensive handmade papers can be difficult to cut as well. Look for cardstock with a smooth finish. Some papers are even polished.

Double-sided cardstock, widely used in this book, is easily available where you find nice paper. It makes for a more finished look, especially when used for making boxes.

Specialty Paper

Specialty papers are fun to experiment with. I love how easily foil papers cut with my machine or scissors. Glitter paper can be messy unless it is coated with a clear finish by the manufacturer that seals the glitter on a colored background. Flocked, embossed, handmade or iridescent papers sometimes require a little extra care in handling or cutting.

Vellum

I use vellum in many of my projects. It is beautiful and soft when lit from behind, making it a must for lanterns. It is nice to write on for tags and cards and lends an interesting layer to paper fashions or flowers. I usually use scissors to cut vellum rather than my machine.

Stencil Board

Stencil, or oil board, is used to make stencils. In order for it to resist paint and remain a sturdy medium, it is saturated with linseed oil and then baked. It has an unmistakable appearance because of the mottling caused by the oil. It doesn't bend well, but it cuts like a dream, though it requires more pressure and two cuts—one to score the surface, a second to cut through. You can use poster board in place of stencil board, but the posterboard does not have anywhere near the strength of the stencil board and may require an additional layer for sturdiness.

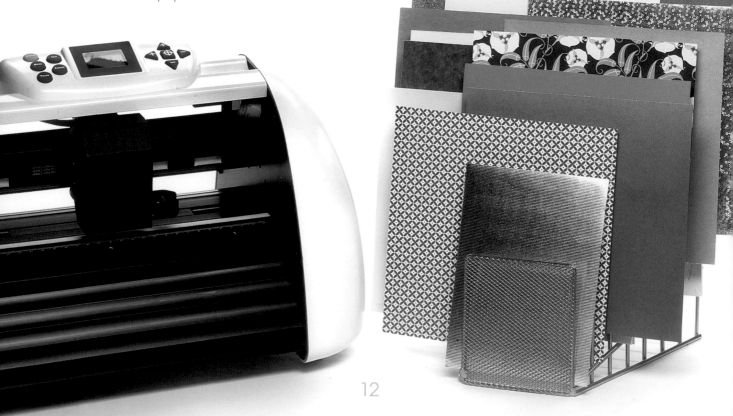

When stencil board is fresh or in bulk, it can smell of linseed oil, but it airs out eventually. I like the smell, though some don't. A nice side effect of the linseed oil is that it keeps blades nice and sharp.

Freezer Paper

Freezer paper is quite thick and comes on a roll. It has a slick coating on one side. Freezer paper makes an excellent work surface cover, especially when working with glue.

Tip

Store all paper and paper projects in a dry place away from sunlight. As with many art media, moisture and UV rays quickly deteriorate paper. Sunlight will also fade paper, ribbon and trims. Moisture can warp or mildew paper, loosen adhesives and dilute dyes.

ELECTRONIC CUTTER

An electronic cutter is an invaluable asset to an art studio or home craft room. I use a Klic-N-Kut MAXX. Other brands include Pazzles, Wishblade and Craft Robo. Choose a machine that suits your needs and budget best. Make sure the cutter is compatible with your computer's operating system and that it has a cutting area of at least 12" × 12".

Look for a cutter that handles the primary materials you want to cut. The Klic-N-Kut MAXX cuts paper, cardstock, cork, foam, heavy stencil and chip board. If you are cutting only paper, cardstock and thin stencil board, this may be more than you need.

The ability to cut fine details in a variety of materials makes a personal cutter a dream to own. The ease with which you can accurately cut multiples makes a cutter an ideal tool for teachers, scout leaders, scrapbooking groups or other organizations.

There is a learning curve to using an electronic cutter, and it is not an inexpensive item. However, I find the expense easy to justify, considering what you can save on purchasing precut paper blanks and embellishments.

BLADES
Electronic Cutter Blades

If your machine's blade starts to make ragged cuts, it likely needs to be replaced (though before running to the store, check your user manual for any adjustments that can be made). Match blades to the manufacturer of the machine you are using.

Generally, you should use the shortest blade possible—only as deep as the paper you use. Use deep-cut blades for stencil board, chip board and heavy specialty papers. Keep blades you're not using capped. They are tiny, but extremely sharp.

Scissors

Scissors are an important tool to have on hand whether you have an electronic cutter or not. Use them for trimming, repairing and embellishing your paper projects. Use decorative scissors to cut scraps into decorative text boxes or give a handmade touch to an invitation insert.

Good scissors used only for paper are a must, though they don't always have to be expensive. Look for trusted brands and a guarantee. I like titanium scissors. They seem to stay sharp longer. Nonstick scissors are great for cutting double-sided tape. Choose scissors that fit your fingers. Scissors 6" (15cm) or smaller offer the best control. A fine, sharp tip aids in clipping tight spots.

Craft Knife and Self-Healing Mat

A good, sharp craft knife consists of a handle with a replaceable blade. If you are doing lots of cutting, choose a knife with a soft grip or add one. It can relieve a lot of stress on your hands.

A self-healing mat goes hand in hand with a craft knife. The material and texture of the mat helps keep the paper from sliding as you cut, and it protects your work surface from cut marks.

ADHESIVES

Adhesive Putty

Soft and pliable, you can knead adhesive putty lightly and stick it between two surfaces for a temporary hold. Adhesive putty will hold a paper castle on the wall or butterflies on a window. You can also use it to hold place mats in place on the table or to keep weights in place, as with the metal washer that weighs down the *Fox Place Card* (see page 40).

Double-Sided Tape

I use double-sided tape extensively in my paper designs. It is a good choice for items with long, straight seams like the handbag or pillow box projects. However, you have to be precise in your placement, because you can't take it off without damaging the paper. Double-sided tape comes in several widths. Terrifically Tacky Tape by Provo Craft holds glass beads, glitter and other embellishments particularly well.

Fabric Paint

I like to use fabric paint as an adhesive as well as a decorative element. You can add fine dimensional details by applying paint and dusting it with glitter, or you can set small stones with a bead of fabric paint.

Foam Tape

I use foam tape, or mounting tape, for three-dimensional effects. It makes silhouette flowers bloom and vases stand out. The foam layer has adhesive on both sides and the tape comes in circles, squares, dots and other shapes.

Glue

Liquid glue is a must for paper projects. You can apply it directly from the bottle nozzle or with a card or toothpick. Clean any excess glue off your materials with a paper towel or soft cloth for a professional finish. White and tacky glues should be left to dry completely before you continue work.

Aleene's Original Tacky Glue is my real workhorse glue. It buckles some papers if applied too thickly, but on the whole, it works well on many types of paper and mixed-media materials. I use it to assemble pieces and add feathers, trims, rhinestones and pearls. The gel version works just as well as the original. My favorite thing about this brand is that there is no noxious smell.

Tools

Awl

Use an awl to curl paper. If you don't have an awl, you can use a tool with a round handle, such as a paintbrush, pen, pencil, knitting needle or dowel instead. Awls and handles of different diameters make different sized curls.

Bone Folder

A bone folder is a flat instrument, usually 6" (15cm) long, resembling a tongue depressor. Once made of whale bone, bone folders are now made of a synthetic plastic. They have a pointed end and a rounded end. The pointed end helps make creases and folds.

Hole Punch

There are many different sizes and shapes of punches. If you cut silhouettes by hand, punches can help you make many of the interior cuts that a machine cutter would otherwise handle.

Needle Tool

Often found among clay tools at retail stores, a needle tool can aid you in removing paper elements from your electronic cutter's adhesive mat. Slide the needle end under the edge of the paper and slowly lift. It helps to release very detailed cuts like tree branches. A needle tool also serves well as a precise applicator for glue. Dried glue slips right off the metal needle.

Pencil and Eraser

A pencil should be a part of every silhouette artist's toolbox. In addition to using the eraser to eliminate marks made by the pencil, you can use it to hold down two items that you're in the process of gluing together.

Pliers

Round nose pliers have round, pointed ends ideal for making loops in wire.

Pounce Wheel

Found in the sewing department, a perforating pounce wheel consists of a spiked wheel with a handle. Designed to punch tiny holes in tissue paper for pattern-making, you can use the pounce wheel to make fold lines in your silhouettes.

Ruler

A ruler is another staple for silhouette artistry. With a ruler, you can measure and draw straight lines. You can also make crisp folds by placing the edge of the ruler at the fold and bending the paper around it. You can smooth out the fold with the edge of the ruler.

Wire Cutters and Rosary Pliers

Wire cutters, or nippers, are hand tools that snip wire. Rosary pliers combine, in one tool, the fine, round tip of round nose pliers with the ability to snip wire.

Embellishments

Glitter

It is amazing how many colors of glitter are available today. Use a sheet of paper folded in half to catch excess glitter. When you're done, funnel the glitter back into the container. Once the glitter application is dry, tap the back side of the area that has been glittered to shake off the excess.

I like to use custom mixes of glitter, so instead of putting glitter back in its old container when I'm done using it, I put it in a new container with several other colors or types of glitter.

Microbeads

Tiny, no-hole glass beads add a sophisticated touch to paper crafts. Apply them as you would glitter. If using large microbeads, sprinkle some fine glitter over the beads to fill in spaces between the beads with sparkle.

Pens, Colored Pencils, Markers, Stamps

Experiment with drawing or painting on paper silhouettes to express yourself more fully. Try out a calligraphy pen on invitations, gel pens to add color or a metallic pen for a touch of elegance.

Ribbon

Always in style, ribbon adds a tactile aspect to paper art. Apply ribbon with double-sided tape, fabric glue or tacky glue. Use it to hang lanterns, embellish cards or string tags.

Scale

Scale is an important design consideration. You can make a flower large enough for use as a wall accent or small enough to add the perfect touch to a paper doll dress. You can cut it to use as a place mat or scale it down for use on a greeting card floral arrangement. Experiment with scale and repetition. One tree can make a striking statement on a card or in a window. Five trees, on a smaller, slimmer scale, make a forest. One large leaf is bold, while many small falling leaves are poetic. A simple geometric shape makes for an op-art or retro design when you use it in many different scales together.

Some Uses for Small-Scale Elements

Small-scale elements work well for cards, scrapbooking, window views, doll or dollhouse items and magnets. I like to make miniatures to tuck into packages and cards or to toss about as an accent to a special table setting. When cut a little larger than confetti, a tiny version of a moon or a butterfly makes a fun surprise, especially if it reflects the motif of the card, gift or party.

Some Uses for Large-Scale Elements

Larger-scale designs can be used as place mats, announcements, and window and wall décor. You should reinforce larger items in some way if you expect them to be handled or played with. For this reason, some designs include reinforcements in places where stress is anticipated. For many designs, I've suggested using a heavier paper stock.

Sizing Elements for Projects

The cutting designs contained on the CD accompanying the book, when cut at actual size, will fit on either $8\frac{1}{2}$" × 11" or 12" x 12" paper or cardstock. You will need to adjust the paper size if you change the scale of any of the elements. If you make design elements smaller, you'll have no problem fitting them on one of the above paper sizes and may even be able to fit several elements on the same page. However, if you make designs larger, you will need to make sure the electronic cutter or printer you are using can handle the larger paper dimensions required.

You will notice that, often, the same cutting design is used in numerous projects in different scales. For instance, in the photo at left, the Shoe Set elements are cut very small for confetti and a little larger for the *Shoe Card* (page 85). Choose the size you'd like to make your project, then scale the main design element of the project first. Adjust the size of the other elements appropriately.

When scaling entire design sets, (such as the Doll Ornament Set on page 121), scale the entire set by the same percentage—if the doll is reduced to 75%, the dress should be at 75%, too. The lantern sets should be cut at 100% if you intend to fit a tea light inside.

Gluing

When gluing pieces together, especially long seams, it helps to weigh down the area being glued as it dries. Weighing down items will help you to achieve smooth, strong seams without buckling or wrinkling. If the design does not fold in half, weigh down just the seam and not the entire item. Before weighing down, make sure to remove excess glue. Use a toothpick as a tool. It is best to let glue dry slightly before trying to remove the excess to ensure the least amount of mess.

Put baking parchment or freezer paper between the paper project and the weight. Either will help to ensure any remaining glue does not stick to your weight. It will also help keep the surface of the project clean. Place freezer paper slick side down.

Some items I like to use as weights include:

- Glass squares or discs (look for thick, flat glass shapes in candle departments)
- A heavy book
- Sewing weights
- Heavy coasters

You can also add weights to projects to help you display them. I use them to make things like paper doll stands and place card holders. For this purpose, I tend to use:

- Washers
- Coins
- Rocks

Cutting

USING THE CD DESIGNS

The CD included with this book features designs you can cut either by hand or by using an electronic die-cutting machine. To access the files on your computer, insert the CD into your CD-ROM drive. The files are in .eps and .pdf formats, so you will need a graphics program such as Adobe Illustrator or Adobe Photoshop to open the .eps files and a program such as Adobe Reader to open the .pdf files.

CUTTING ELECTRONICALLY

You can cut the designs on the CD using an electronic die-cutting machine. Machines vary in the types of files they will import, so check the manual to make sure yours can import .eps files. Follow the manufacturer's instructions for using the files.

When using a machine to cut your silhouettes, keep the blade pressure low to start and the speed slow. Slow speed always gives better results, particularly on detailed cuts. Pressure can be added until you get a nice, clean cut.

CUTTING BY HAND

If you don't have an electronic die-cutting machine, you can cut designs by hand. To cut the designs on the CD, import the files into your graphics or reader program and then print the outline in color on the back of the paper you are to cut. Use scissors or a sharp craft knife and a self-healing cutting mat. Do not cut the fold lines marked in blue in the original files. Fold them by hand after you've finished cutting.

TIPS FOR CUTTING

When cutting with either a machine or regular scissors, keeping the following things in mind will help you to make the most of your time and supplies:

- Use sharp blades. It makes a big difference in precision cutting.
- Keep blades sharp by cutting only one material with them. In this case, paper.
- You can sharpen scissors, blades and punches by cutting aluminum foil. Lubricate them by cutting wax paper.
- Place elements close together when you cut to make the most of your paper. Save scraps for title boxes and paper ribbons, or collect them to give to an art class. I give mine to an artist who makes paper.
- My best advice for either type of cutting: Go slow. You will get more accurate cut lines and less snagging of edges.
- Use mini zipper bags for storing and organizing small cut elements. Use scrapbooking paper keepers or see-through snap envelopes for larger cuts.

Intricate Hand Cutting

Some of my designs feature a lot of detail and require extra care when cutting by hand. Here are some helpful hints to make the challenge easier.

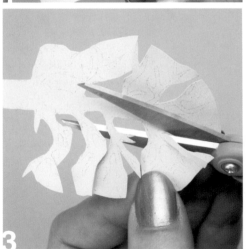

1. Cut off a single image to work with. Trim it down close to the outline. Cut with the part of the blades nearest to the handle, avoiding using the tips of the blades. Only use the tips when you get down to the very small details. Manipulate the paper as well as the scissors to change angles.

2. Trim the item down to the outside edges of the smallest outer details so that there is very little excess paper left.

3. Cut the main sections out first and the smallest details last, whittling the silhouette down as you go. This puts less stress on the paper.

4. When you have a sharp angle to cut, cut in from one side, then cut in from the other. If you're cutting and the paper starts to show a lot of resistance, go at it from another angle.

Note

For the most part, the materials lists for the projects in the following chapters assume the use of an electronic cutter. Therefore, the additional tools you might need to hand cut and fold a project (such as scissors and a pounce wheel) are not listed. Plan accordingly.

5. Use the tips of the scissors to snip small details. Sometimes you'll end up with a little hanging tab. Go at it from the opposite side to cut it away.

6. Finish trimming any ends intended to be pointed with a few, final snips.

7. When cutting an element with a craft knife, leave a bigger margin of paper around it than you would if you were using scissors. This gives you more to hold onto. Start cutting the branches from the inside angles and work your way out.

8. Use the index finger of your free hand to hold the paper in place directly in front of your blade.

Tip

When cutting with a craft knife, cut with the tip of the blade at a slight angle, with a firm, even pressure. Practice making curves and corners on scrap paper.

Punches

Use punches to make basic shapes like circles and ovals. Match the punches you have to the design elements in the projects like flowers, butterflies or stars. Punching basic shapes from scraps is a great way to use as much of your paper as possible.

You can use many punches upside down. Not only is it easier on the hands to push down on the punch frame, you can also see exactly where you are punching.

Many punches come with a hinged grip that allows you to punch with one hand while you hold the paper with the other. They require just a small amount of pressure at the base.

Cutouts

Some designs have detailed cutouts inside the silhouette outline (like the *Pillow Box Purse 2* handle on page 123). I use a combination of a hole punch and scissors to manage these by hand.

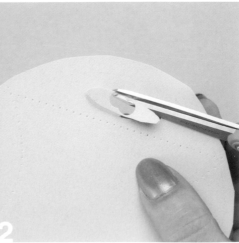

1. To cut interior details, the easiest thing to do is to first punch a hole or two inside the area of the detail to give an opening for scissors and avoid stressing the paper.

2. Insert your scissors in the hole you punched and begin to cut the opening.

Folding

I sometimes use a pounce wheel to make fold lines when hand cutting. It creates a perforated line much as the electronic cutter does with dashed cuts. Such perforations are especially helpful for curved folds. Go slow and use a guide. You will get a nice, easy-to-use fold line.

1. Trim away all excess paper from the design. Make perforations along straight fold lines with a tracing or pounce wheel and ruler.

2. Use a rounded dish or other object to guide the pounce wheel when making curved fold lines. It's alright if the arc isn't exactly perfect.

3. If you need to make curved fold lines a little more defined, follow along them with your fingernail, applying pressure as you go.

Stacked Designs

Several designs can be stacked or layered for dimensional interest. The cherry blossom, deer and ribbons and banners are good examples of this. They can be used alone as a silhouette or with the additional detail files like petals or cushions.

CHERRY BLOSSOM

The *Cherry Blossom* motif makes a lovely card front or piece of framed art when layered with colorful papers. It also works well as an element in lanterns or backgrounds when cut as a solid shape.

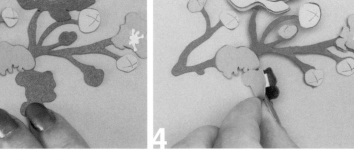

1. Glue the single petal on the large blossom and the open blossom.

2. Add the buds and the center of the cherry blossom.

3. Add the first piece of the leaf to the stem.

4. Using foam tape, add the top petals of the two blossoms and the leaf.

GRAPHIC FILES: Cherry Blossom Set

Deer

Made in two pieces, this deer can stand alone if you add a hinge. Foam tape separates the sides just enough to give it dimension. Use the deer on cards, as a name tag, in lanterns or as wall decor.

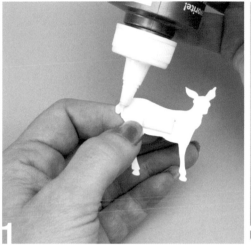 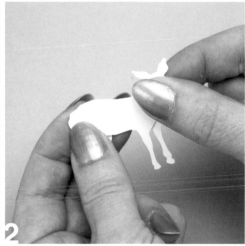

1. Put foam tape on one of the deer pieces. Put a dab of glue on both the tail and the head.

2. Position the second deer piece on top, matching up the head and the tail (the rest of the pieces aren't intended to match up perfectly).

Graphic Files: Deer Set

Ribbons and Banners

Paper ribbons can be made from strips of paper scraps. Cut strips in different widths and layer them for a classic trim. Trim boxes, paper doll clothes, cards and tags. Banners make a special touch for the front of an envelope, card, mobile or gift box. Make a large one for a sign or door plate. The soft curling of the edges helps convey the banner effect.

 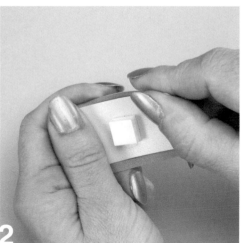

1. Cut paper scraps into strips of different widths. Apply double-sided tape or glue to each strip and place one on top of another to create a decorative paper ribbon.

2. For a banner, use shorter strips and, after gluing, bend the center to create a curve. Bend the two ends back. Smooth out the bend to get rid of crimps. Stack two pieces of foam tape in the center of the back of the banner.

CHAPTER TWO

Party Pieces

Whether you're hosting or attending a party, these festive party pieces will surely impress. Make gift boxes, cards and tags to take to a party. Create coordinating napkin rings, a mobile and place cards to throw a memorable soirée.

There are so many design elements included on the CD that it is easy to customize a gift or party presentation to your own style and personality. Use the color combinations I have used or come up with your own.

Projects shown: Gusset Purse (page 37), Pillow Box (page 26), Retro Home Place Card (page 44), Pillow Box Purse (page 31)

Pillow Box

The pillow box is popular in specialty stores for gift giving because of its unusual shape and pop-open feature. Pair a one-of-a-kind box with torn tissue paper and you have packaging that shows true thoughtfulness.

When popped into form, the pillow box provides surprising protection for its contents, even when cut from thin cardstock, because of its convex shape. It stores flat and assembles with one seam.

MATERIALS & TOOLS
Double-sided cardstock
Tacky glue or double-sided tape

GRAPHIC FILES
Pillow Box (Don't cut the window.)

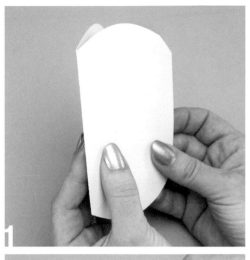

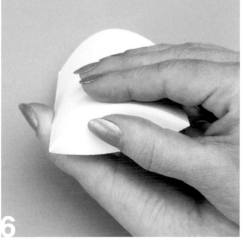

1. Cut out your pillow box. Fold it along the center line.

2. Fold the long tab in.

3. Push along the curved end folds.

4. Add a line of glue on the tab close to the fold line. Even out the glue line so that it's smooth.

5. Fold the sides of the box together so that the other long edge of the box meets the tab line. Press and hold, or weigh it down, until somewhat dry.

6. Once dry, put your thumb inside one end of the box to pop it open. Fold in both flaps of one end. Repeat for the other side. To open the box, open the flaps at one end.

Note

The bigger the box, the thicker the paper should be. You can bolster a larger box with tissue paper and the paper needs to stay in place if the box is to be saved as your box will be!

Pillow Box with Flap

This design has a decorative flap that neatly hides the ends of the handmade paper ribbon. I like to finish the box with a glittery eyelet and a bold brad. Use an earth-tone eyelet instead of the glittery pink here to make a gift box for *him*.

MATERIALS & TOOLS

Double-sided cardstock

Paper ribbon about 6" (15cm) long (see page 23)

Tacky glue

Small hole punch

Large metal brad

Colorful string

GRAPHIC FILES

Circle

Pillow Box Purse 2 (Do not make interior handle cut.)

1. Assemble the box (see steps 1 and 2 for the *Pillow Box* on page 27). The seam of the box is glued at the fold of the flap. Punch a small hole in the center of the front flap.

2. Puff out the box and turn down the flap, folding the end flaps in at the same time.

3. Break the grain of the ribbon and curve it.

4. Put a line of glue on the back of the ribbon. Fold the flap of the purse in place and adhere the ribbon just under the flap, centering it on the front of the box.

5. At the bottom of the gift box, bend the ribbon back towards itself, making a fold line.

6. Bring the ribbon all the way around the back of the box, adhering it as you go. Bend the ribbon back for a second fold line where the flap meets the top of the box.

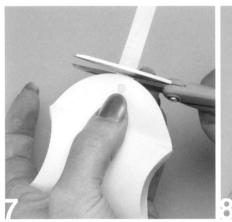
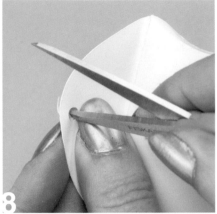

7. Trim the ribbon from the back. That way you can see and follow the curve of the flap as you cut the trim. Turn the box over and see how neatly it matches.

8. Use the tips of a pair of scissors to create a hole in the ribbon that matches up with the hole in the flap of the purse.

9. Make a colorful eyelet by punching a hole in the center of a circle. Place the eyelet over the hole on top of the ribbon and secure it with a brad. Take some cord and pull it under the brad. Secure the string by tying it around the brad's post.

Note

When filling gift boxes with chocolate or something crumbly like fudge, line the box with parchment paper or place the goodies in a mini zipper bag to avoid saturating the box with oils. Finish with a layer of torn tissue paper.

Party Cone Favor Boxes

Cut without windows, the *Hanging Cone Lantern* (see page 111) doubles as a gift box, or this elegant box can be filled with scented crystals and hang it in a bedroom. To add a tassel for interest and movement, glue it into the seam at the bottom of the cone.

SUPPLIES: Double-sided cardstock, double-sided tape, tacky glue, small decorative metal clip, ribbon, acrylic gems

GRAPHIC FILES: Triangle Lantern Set (Triangle Lantern)

Tip

Roll tissue paper into a cone shape to insert into the box as a liner. Use baking parchment as a liner if you are giving an oily treat like chocolate.

Pillow Box Purses

These variations on the *Pillow Box* make miniature paper purses to fill with a sweet gem of a gift for the girly girl or the fashion maven. Keep it simple or kick it up with bright, modern motifs.

SUPPLIES: Double-sided cardstock, metallic or pearl paper, tacky glue, rhinestones, glitter

GRAPHIC FILES: Pillow Box Purse 1 or 2, assorted decorative motifs

Fox Party Gift Box

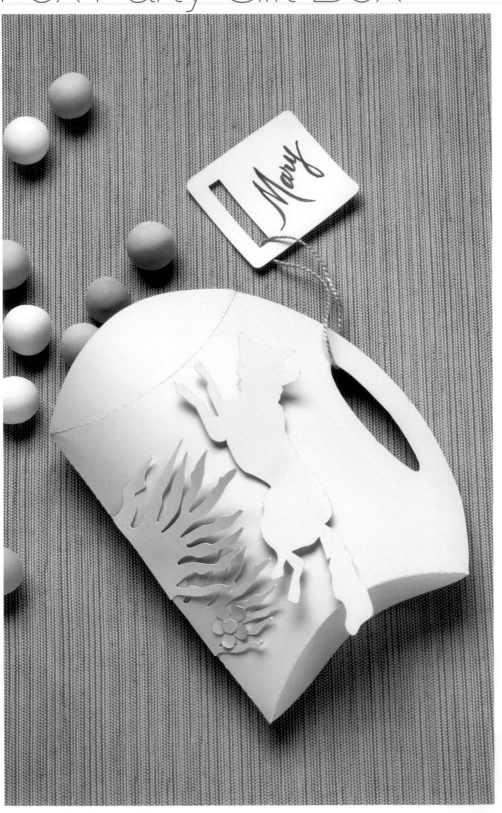

Guests will feel honored when they find a gift inside this handled pillow box. Add a simple tag and it is a uniquely personal presentation. Fill with candies, paper items like stars, butterflies or tags, or a ticket to an event. What will you put inside?

MATERIALS & TOOLS
Double-sided cardstock
Tacky glue
Fine-tip black pen
Green string

GRAPHIC FILES
Flower Set D (FD4)
Fox
Pillow Box Purse 2
Seaweed Set (Cut 2 of 4.)
Tag no. 15

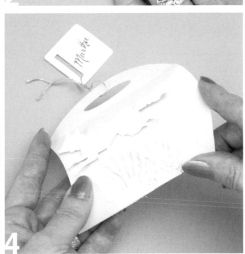

1. Assemble a pillow box purse (see instructions for the *Pillow Box with Flap* on page 29). Leave the handle tab unfolded and unglued. Add a couple layers of seaweed, a flower and then a fox jumping over the assembly.

2. Write a person's name on a tag and attach the string.

3. Use the string to tie the tag to the handle of the box. Be careful not to tie too tightly or you may rip the paper.

4. Push the end flaps connected to the back of the box in first and the front flaps in last toward the back of the box.

Party Kits

You can use these boxes to make gift kits. Collect multiple sets of all the elements needed to make a particular paper gift—beads and elastic, paper flowers that already have double-sided tape on the back or paper dolls in miniature. Place sets of items in mini zipper bags. Put each bag in a box. Boxes with handles, such as this one, are especially fun for on-the-go projects, such as a sleepover or a car trip. The party favor becomes a party activity when you turn a box into a kit.

Gusset Box

The gusset is the fold that gives this box its unique shape and flexibility. The box has a handle that can be threaded with ribbon or cord for a decorative bow or as a hanging loop. Cut it small for little gifts or larger for candies, earrings or to fill with paper gifts. This sweet box has a little lock tab to stay closed.

MATERIALS & TOOLS
Double-sided cardstock
Tacky glue or double-sided tape

GRAPHIC FILES
Gusset Box

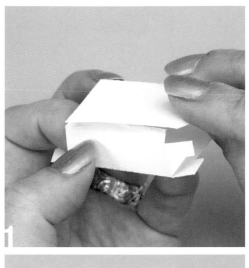

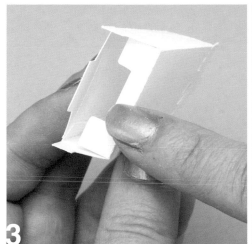

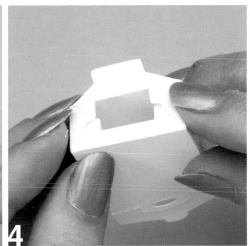

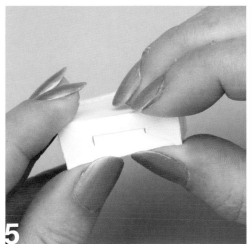

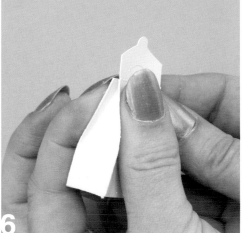

1. Cut out your gusset box. Fold along the fold lines, creating a box shape, but leave the gusset lines (the V folds on the sides of the box) unfolded for now.

2. Glue the long side flap closed. Hold it shut for a few seconds.

3. Fold in the long bottom flap with the slot.

4. Fold in the short bottom flaps.

5. Fold in the last bottom flap so that it locks down the other ones.

6. Pinch down the gusset fold lines on both sides.

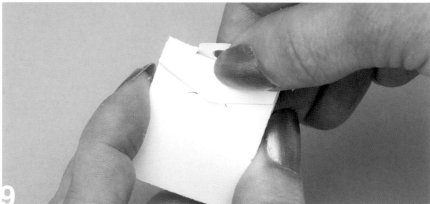

7. Push out the tab on the back of the box.

8. Use your fingernail to push open the little slot on the front of the box.

9. Fold the box top tab into the slot.

How to Finish a Gift Box

Cut several pieces of tissue paper big enough to extend past the opening of the box. Tuck one or two pieces gently into the box. Use a pencil, eraser down, as a tool, if you need help getting the paper in place. Wrap the gift in a piece of paper, push it into the box, and tuck the ends of all the sheets of tissue paper inside.

For added drama:

• Use several different colors of tissue paper.

• Add paper, cellophane or metallic shreds to the paper.

• Throw in little cuts of flowers, circles or stars amid the layers for surprise after surprise.

• Tie ribbon around the paper holding the gift, especially if the gift is fragile or small.

• Add a gift tag or medallion with the name of the intended recipient.

• Add a piece of chocolate or rose petals to the gift.

Tooth Fairy Boxes

When my daughter Natalie (mother of five) saw the tiny boxes littering my studio she proclaimed, "Tooth fairy boxes!" So this project is dedicated to her and her tribe. Place a washed and dried baby tooth in tissue paper inside a small box. Have the child help to package it. Close the box with a metal clip. Write your child's name and age on tags cut from coordinating cardstock. In the morning, the little box will have flown away and the tooth fairy will have left a prize beneath the pillow.

SUPPLIES: Double-sided cardstock, metallic paper, tacky glue, miniature decorative metal clip, glitter, ribbon, string

GRAPHIC FILES: Fairy Wings or Angel Wings 1 or 3, Gusset Box or Triangle Lantern Set (Triangle Lantern), Tooth, assorted tags

Gusset Purse

The Gusset Purse is adapted from the Gusset Box. The tab is elongated for style, a handle is added and the buckle is just plain fun.

SUPPLIES: Double-sided cardstock, metallic paper, tacky glue

GRAPHIC FILES: Buckle Set (B14), Gusset Purse Set

Butterfly Napkin Ring

A lighthearted accent to a place setting, these paper napkin rings are pretty and easy to make. It is a project that can easily utilize scrap paper. Try making napkin rings with flowers, shoes or a fox. Match the motif to the party theme you have chosen. Napkin rings are the only decoration needed to make any dinner special.

MATERIALS & TOOLS

Double-sided cardstock

Paper ribbon about 5" (13cm) long (See page 23 for instructions.)

Tacky glue

Awl

Cylindrical object, such as a glue bottle

GRAPHIC FILES

Butterfly Set (Butterfly 1 and Butterfly Body)

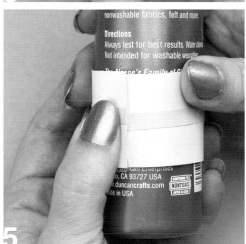

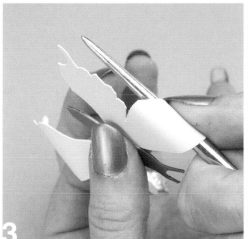
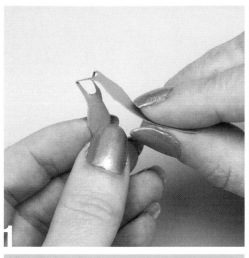
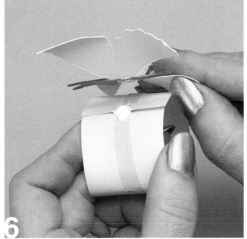

1. Fold the butterfly body in half at the antennae.

2. Put glue on one inside half of the butterfly body. Adhere the body to the back of the butterfly. Apply glue to the front inside of the butterfly and fold the body down.

3. Curl the wings with an awl or pencil. This step is optional. For a cleaner, simpler look leave the wings uncurled as shown in the photo on page 38.

4. Fold the wings up and in toward the body in front.

5. Take a paper ribbon and wrap it around a cylinder (like a glue bottle). Glue the ends together.

6. Put a generous dot of glue in the middle of the napkin ring on the seam. Adhere your butterfly.

Fox Place Card

Your guests will want to save their place cards from this party. The fox stands require a little time and assembly, but the whimsy is worth it. And since each place card is weighted, it will stay put.

MATERIALS & TOOLS

Double-sided cardstock
Adhesive putty
Foam tape
Tacky glue
Fine-tip black pen
Round nose pliers
Coin or metal washer
Green floral stem wire
Dimensional flower
Rhinestone

GRAPHIC FILES

Fox (Cut 2.)
Paper Doll Set (PD Stand 2)
Seaweed

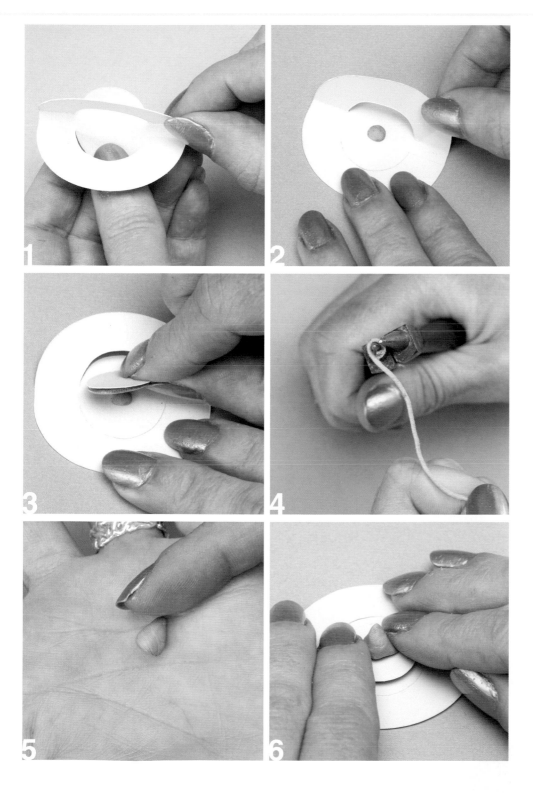

1. Fold the stand along its fold lines.

2. Put a small piece of putty in the center of the inner circle.

3. Put putty on a washer or coin and cover the coin with the separate circle from the stand set. Place the covered coin on the putty in the stand's inner circle.

4. Take a 3" (8cm) length of wrapped floral wire and bend it into curves. Make a loop with your pliers at both ends of the wire.

5. Shape a pea-sized piece of putty into a cone.

6. Place the cone on the weight cover.

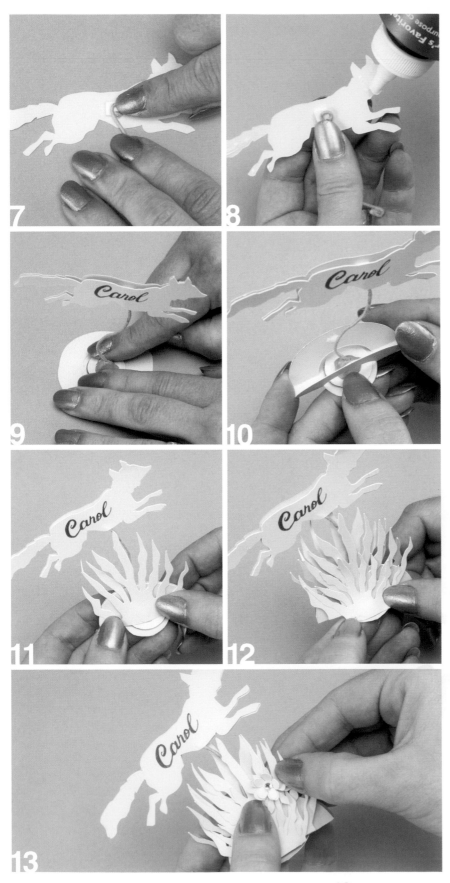

7. Place a piece of foam tape in the center of the fox. Stick one loop of the wire onto the double-sided tape.

8. Put a dot of glue on the fox's head and tail. Write a guest's name on the other fox. Adhere the second fox to the first, matching them up.

9. Place the free end of the floral wire into the cone of putty on the stand and press the putty around the loop, making sure to center it.

10. Add a drop of glue to each side of the stand and press the two arcs together. Let it dry completely.

11. Glue a large piece of seaweed to the front of the stand. Repeat for the back.

12. Glue a smaller piece of seaweed to the stand base over each larger piece of grass.

13. Embellish with a small flower centered with a rhinestone.

SHOE PARTY PLACE CARD AND CONFETTI

What girl doesn't love shoes and handbags? Your favorite shopper will appreciate the detail of shoe place cards at a ladies' party. Coordinate solids with patterned papers easily by buying a themed paper stack. Toss matching shoe silhouettes about for big, bold confetti splashes. It helps to write the name on the card before adhering the shoe in case you make a mistake. I like to finish place cards on both sides so guests are sure to know each other's names. Let the guests take the confetti shoes if they like. Pair each place card with a gusset purse gift box filled with fine candies, a piece of jewelry, lip gloss or a charm.

SUPPLIES: Double-sided cardstock, tacky glue, black fine-tip marker
GRAPHIC FILES: Shoe Set (Shoe 1 and Shoe 1 Upper)

Retro Home Place Cards

The coffee table makes a self-standing place card. Write guests' names on both sides to help them remember each other's names. As if it wasn't enough to be invited to a hip happening, when guests find their places with these stylized table cards, they will feel simply spoiled.

MATERIALS & TOOLS
Double-sided cardstock
Tacky glue

GRAPHIC FILES
Retro Set (Coffee Table—Cut 2.)

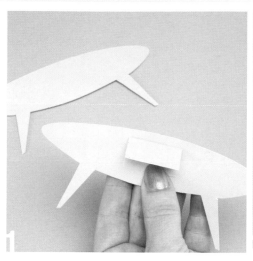

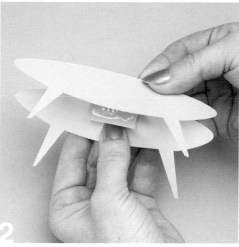

1. Fold a scrap of cardstock or paper in half to make a hinge. Glue the hinge to the center of one of the tables.

2. Put glue on the other side of the hinge and place the other table piece on top.

DEER PLACE CARD

The deer place card is simple yet stunning. It makes a nice accent to a lantern for a beautiful winter theme. Use the instructions for assembling the deer on page 23 for a reference. Rather than adding foam tape between the two layers, adhere a paper hinge as for the *Retro Home Place Cards*. Write your guest's name on the deer's body. Notice how the front and the back of the deer are different to make for a dimensional look when standing.

SUPPLIES: Double-sided cardstock, scrap paper or cardstock, tacky glue, permanent fine-tip marker

GRAPHIC FILES: Deer Set

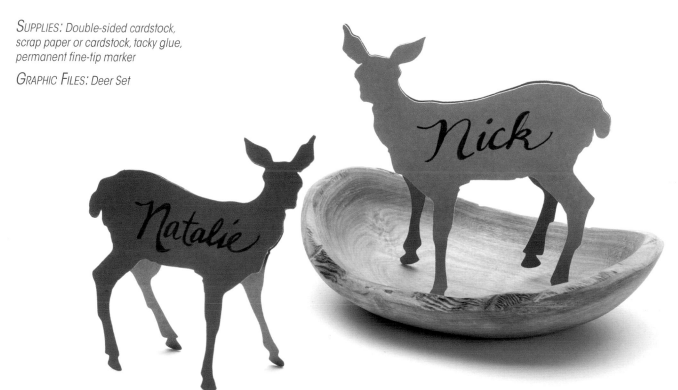

Mermaid Tag

A bronzy mermaid, vellum and paper flora make a cool gift tag with a touch of glitz. Using vellum as an overlay takes the pressure off—if you make a mistake, just cut another scrap of vellum with fancy-edges scissors and start over.

MATERIALS & TOOLS
Double-sided cardstock

Vellum

Tacky glue

Deckle-edged scissors

Fine-tip black pen

Glitter

Pearl

Silky cord

GRAPHIC FILES
Ferns

Flower Set D (FD4)

Mermaid

Tag Set (Tag 17)

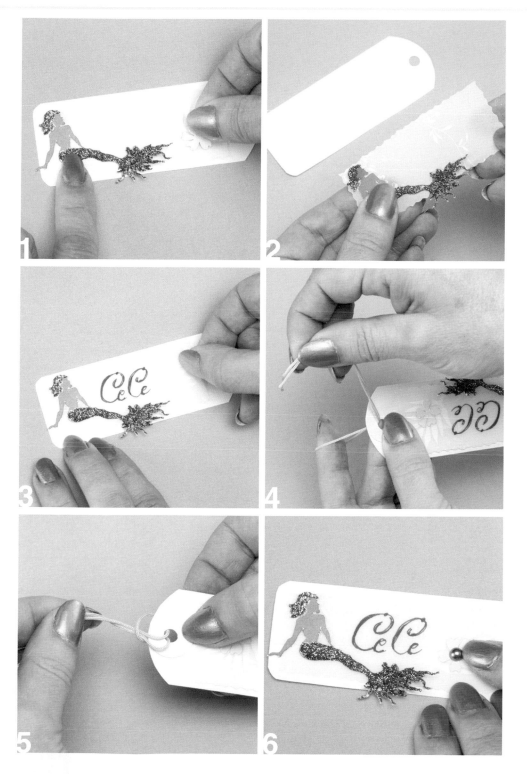

1. Decorate your mermaid's tail and hair with glitter. Cut the edges of the vellum with decorative scissors. Compose the entire gift tag before you start to adhere elements.

2. Adhere the background pieces to the tag with glue. Add the mermaid to the vellum, placing it so that you have lots of room to write.

3. Place small dots of glue on the corners of the vellum and adhere it to the tag. Add final embellishments on top.

4. Add paper eyelet reinforcers to both sides of the hole. To make a reinforcer, simply punch a small hole inside a larger paper circle. Finish with ribbon or cord. Fold a cord (or two cords) in half and feed the top loop through the hole with the loop toward the back and the loose ends to the front.

5. Thread the ends of the cord through the loop at the other end.

6. Add a rhinestone or pearl.

CHAPTER THREE

Art

Imagine an underwater fantasy, a personal angel to adorn a door or a flying fairy. Make paper playthings like paper dolls with clothes and accessories. Craft paper flowers to adorn hair, walls or boxes. Assemble tokens like the paper locket charm that really opens. Frame dimensional scenes or a single dress with layered trim for unique shadow box art.

Coordinate the colors of your framed art to complement your bedroom, dorm room or a favorite space. If you are giving framed art as a gift and are unsure about the predominant colors of the recipient's room, use neutral or subtle metallic shades that go with a variety of décor. Come up with your own palette by borrowing colors from another source, such as a favorite fabric, rug or painting. Pick the color that you most like in the item and use it as a base color. Use the rest of the colors as accents.

Projects shown: Altered Couture variation (page 61), Dimensional Flower (page 64), Medallion (page 67), Fairy Ornament (page 55), Frameable Fashion variation (page 56), Locket (page 68), Framed Mermaid Art (page 62)

Paper Dolls

This is one versatile young lady. She can be made tall or small—as long as her clothes fit. My specially designed stand can be weighted to hold her in place while she is styling. She should be printed on the front of the paper sheet to be cut, rather than the back. Use the face I've designed as a template to color as you choose or draw your own face. Backed with thin but strong stencil board, this is a doll you can really play with. Cut her clothes from light cardstock or specialty papers.

MATERIALS & TOOLS

Heavy drawing paper, such as bristol

Stencil board

Scrap paper

Tacky glue

Assorted stamps

Chalk ink with pad

Colored pencils

Fabric Paint

Glitter

Micro marbles

Pearls (optional)

Rhinestones (optional)

Ribbon (optional)

GRAPHIC FILES

Paper Doll Set (PD dress 7, PD front [Cut 2—1 from drawing paper, 1 from stencil board.], PD head [optional])

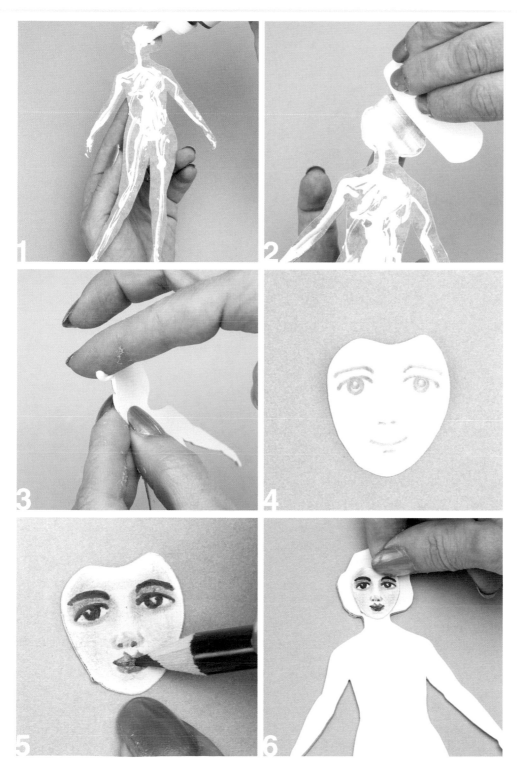

1. Cut one doll from stencil board for the backing and one from drawing paper for the doll front. Coat the entire surface of the backing with liquid glue.

2. Use a piece of card as a squeegee to make sure the glue is smooth. Make sure you get glue on the doll's hands and to the very edges.

3. Adhere the doll front to the doll back and let dry for several seconds. Carefully run your finger along the edges to remove excess glue, making sure not to get any on the front of the doll.

4. Draw your own doll's face in pencil, then pen, or print out the PD Head with facial features already designed.

5. Decorate the face with colored pencil. Use flesh tones in various shades to give her features depth.

6. Adhere the face to the doll. Be careful not to mar her facial features with sticky glue fingers.

51

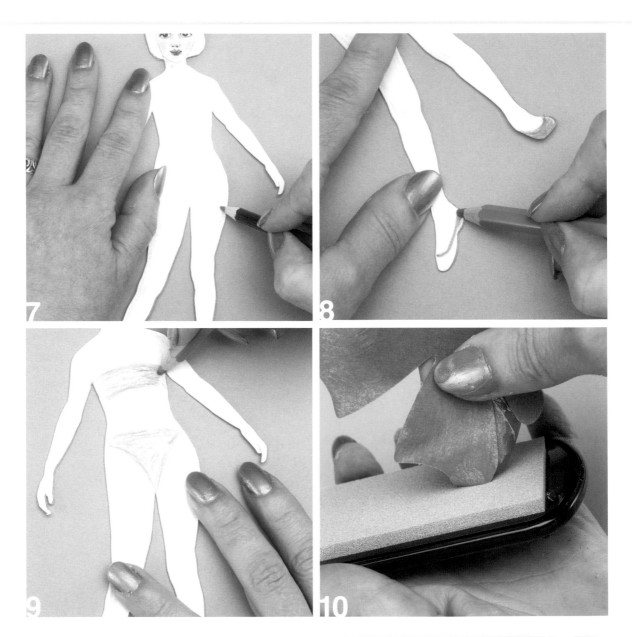

7. Add dimension by shading the edges of the doll's body with a brown pencil.

8. Decorate the doll with clothes. Consider adding slippers, funky undergarments or a neutral leotard.

9. Shade the edges of the undergarments with the same color you used to shade the doll's skin.

10. Hold a piece of clothing between your thumb and forefinger. Swipe it across the ink pad to add a splash of color.

Tip

If using the tutu design with a divided skirt, draw a matching or neutral leotard on your doll, as her undergarments will show.

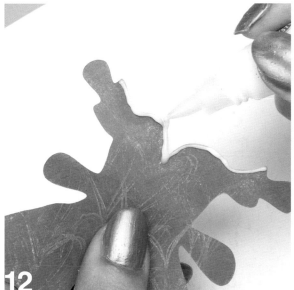

Tip

I like to put a piece of scrap paper beneath items that I am stamping to keep my work surface clean. You can use the same piece of paper to catch excess glitter and micro marbles as you add them.

Tip

With all the wardrobe elements available on the CD included with this book, you will never lack for design possibilities. Try cutting clothing designs from different papers—glittered, satin, printed or foiled. Add fabric, ribbon and feather trims. Use glitter and micro marbles for dazzling embellishments.

11. Stamp a design onto the clothing with a different color ink. Keep stamping until the stamp is clean.

12. Draw designs on with dimensional fabric paint.

13. Sprinkle with glitter and shake off any excess.

14. If using two colors of glitter, shake off the first color before adding the glue for the second. Tap off the excess of the second color.

15. You can also add glue for micro marbles (one of my favorite supplies) as I'm doing on this second dress. Add a generous amount of the marbles.

ANGEL DOOR HANGER

Here is a personal angel to watch over you or someone you love. Make one for someone who needs extra blessing. This project is meant to be one-sided and hung on a surface such as a door or wall. You can finish out the back with circles to cover where the wings are glued on or cut an extra doll in a matching patterned paper to cover the entire back. Remember, if you want the pattern to show on the back, you need to cut the doll in reverse.

SUPPLIES: *Stencil board, cardstock, tacky glue, glitter, ribbon, acrylic stones, monofilament*

GRAPHIC FILES: *Angel Wing Set (Wing 1), Banner Set (BAN 4), Circle, Doll Ornament Set (DO Back, DO Bodice 2, DO Front, DO Skirt 1 [cut 2])*

FANTASY FLYERS

Watch fairies and dragonflies flutter with the slightest breeze. Choose glitter or metallic papers for light-catching fairies and hang them from wooden dowels. Although small children will likely be drawn to these paper fancies, they are not appropriate for little ones to play with because they are delicate. Thin dowels can easily snap and become sharp, creating a safety hazard. To make a fantasy flyer, follow the same process as for assembling the butterfly in the *Mobile* (see page 71), but cut one set of wings and two fairy or dragonfly bodies instead of the butterfly elements. Secure the fishing line between one side of the wings and the body. Secure the line with clear dots of glue centered between the shoulders. Tie the end of the line to a small dowel.

SUPPLIES: Cardstock, patterned paper, tacky glue, monofilament, thin dowel

GRAPHIC FILES: Dragonfly Set (Dragonfly Wings, Dragonfly Body with Legs [Cut 2.]) or Flying Fairy (Cut 2.) and Fairy Wings

FAIRY AND ANGEL ORNAMENTS

For a lovely ornament, assemble a smaller version of the paper doll using the Doll Ornament Set. This doll is in silhouette, so there is no need to draw facial details. For a fairy, finish the back by gluing on wings. Cover the glue joints on the back with scrap paper circles. Finally, add a hanging loop of fishing line to the doll's back.

SUPPLIES: Stencil board, cardstock, patterned and textured paper, tacky glue, ribbon, rhinestone, glitter, 6" (15cm) fishing line or string

GRAPHIC FILES: Angel or Fairy Wings, Doll Ornament Set (DO Back and DO Front), Paper Doll Set (PD Tiara), assorted flowers, assorted dresses

Frameable Fashion

These dimensional fashions make for an exquisite set of paper doll clothes or can be made individually for framing. The layering of paper gives an extra interest to the clothes. Try incorporating other elements from the design templates like bamboo, trees or cats. Have fun playing with style, color and trim.

Materials & Tools
Double-sided cardstock

Paper ribbon

Tacky glue

Awl

Hole punch

Scissors

Rhinestones

Graphic Files
Paper Doll Set (PD dress 2)

Assorted bits and pieces of other design elements to form trim (e.g. brambles, leaves, weeds, assorted flowers)

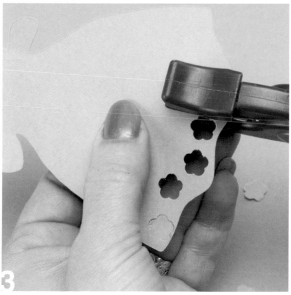

1. Tear up some of your cuts to create small bits that can form lace. I like to use bits of weeds or seaweed.

2. Adhere the bits and pieces to the back of the dress at the collar to create a lace trim. Let it dry.

3. Punch decorative holes near the hem of the dress (save the punched elements for later use).

4. Lay the dress with its holes over a contrasting piece of paper. Trim the paper to fit the dress.

Tip

Frameable Fashion is a creative way to utilize imperfect cuts, scraps and odds and ends. Reimagine bits and pieces as lace, brooches, belts and other adornments.

5. Adhere the paper to the back of the dress so it shows through the holes but not around the edges.

6. Add lace trim to the hem of the dress from the back so that it shows underneath the bottom hem on the front.

7. Turn the dress over. Compose your design. It's easiest to start at the waistline. Put a line of glue across the waist of the dress. Lay the elements into the glue. You can cover the glue and ends with trim later so they won't show.

8. Punch some flowers or other designs out of the contrasting paper. Poke an awl into the center of each cutout to give it some dimension.

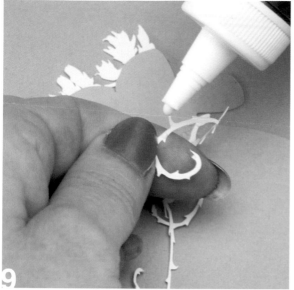

9. Add dots of glue sparingly on other areas of the front of the dress to adhere elements that don't cross the waistline. You can also add dots of glue directly to the elements before placing them.

10. If a punched element isn't quite working, cover it with another element, such as this flower.

11. Adhere the dimensional punched elements. Leave the waistline free of these so that a paper ribbon belt (see page 23) can be added smoothly.

12. Fold back the tabs on the sides of the dress (or cut them off if you're going to frame the dress). Cut a length of ribbon (paper or real) a little larger than the waist. Apply glue to the back of the waistband. Lay in place and let it dry.

Take Risks!

This project is an opportunity to play. Open your imagination to see a fern as an element to repeat, creating a fancy trim. Have some blank dresses at the ready when cleaning your work area. It's a fun way to quickly get inspired and discover unusual combinations.

13. Turn the dress over, making sure that the tabs are out of the way, and trim the waistband from the back.

14. Add nonpaper embellishments such as glitter, rhinestones or pearls to the front. It's especially nice to add something to the waistband.

15. Put your fingers around the dress sides. With your other hand, push in gently to create a curve and break the grain of the paper.

16. Curl the edges more for emphasis. Bend it past where you want it, since the paper will relax.

17. Place your fingers on both sides of the skirt and press, as you see here, to help the dress curve evenly toward the back.

Tip

You can further accentuate the dress's curve by mounting foam tape on the back of the skirt.

ALTERED COUTURE

You can customize paper doll clothes in so many ways! Trim the edges with wavy-edged scissors or cut your own hem design to personalize a piece of clothing. Cut a skirt short and add part of a feather boa for a totally different look.

SUPPLIES: Assorted cardstock, feather boa, glitter, micro beads

GRAPHIC FILES: Paper Doll Set (PD Dress 2)

Framed Mermaid Art

The mattes framing this mermaid art, cut in various contrasting papers, add dimensional delight. The mermaid seems right at home among the rocks and seaweed. Her underwater lair is visited by a seahorse and adorned with pearl seashells.

MATERIALS & TOOLS
Double-sided cardstock

Foam tape

Clear glue dots

GRAPHIC FILES
Coral Set (Coral 2 [Cut several.])

Mermaid

Mermaid Matte Set (MM 1, MM2 and MM3)

Mermaid Perch

Seahorse

Seashell (Cut several.)

Seaweed (Cut Several.)

1. Adhere all three mats together with foam tape. Use foam tape to adhere the background paper behind the mats.

2. Piece together the mermaid scene elements with clear glue dots, starting with the coral. Add the seaweed and rocks.

3. Place the mermaid's perch. Place the mermaid.

4. Crimp the fold lines on the body of the seashell before placing it.

5. Punch out the hole in the seashell.

6. Finally, add the smaller elements, such as the seahorse and seashells.

Dimensional Flowers

Flowers are always in style. A versatile motif, paper flowers have lots of uses. Use them on cards, packages, magnets or as table or hair ornaments. Leave them flat for a graphic look or pinch, roll and stack them for paper flowers that bloom. Make them teeny-tiny for doll or dollhouse accessories. Make them big and bold for wall décor. Stick them on a lampshade. Make a bunch for partygoers to wear as boutonnières. Stack one petal design in different sizes or mix them up and make your own fantastic flowers. Add centers with a paper dot, glitter or a rhinestone.

MATERIALS & TOOLS
Double-sided cardstock
Tacky glue
Awl
Acrylic gem

GRAPHIC FILES
Assorted flowers (Mod Flower shown)

1. Begin with three flower design pieces in different sizes (for this example, the two bottom ones are the same size). Place a dot of glue in the center of the bottom flower's petals.

2. Take the second flower of the same size and lay it on top of the other.

3. Turn it so that its petals fill in the spaces between the petals of the flower below.

4. Put a dot of glue in the center of the flower you just added. Lay the last, smallest flower on top and press.

5. Hold the flower with your thumbnail on the center. Take your other thumbnail and push up all the petals from the bottom layer.

6. Repeat for the top petals.

7. Turn the flower over. Bend the petals around a round tool such as an awl, knitting needle or pencil. This breaks the grain of the paper. If you want to turn the petals upward, use the same technique but curl toward yourself instead of away.

8. You can also crimp the petals, as I'm doing here on a larger flower. Take a petal, put your thumbnail in its center and push.

9. Pinch the ends of the petals. Finish the flower by placing a final flower in a different color plus an acrylic gem, a micro marble, glitter, stones or a paper circle in its center.

Note

The floral set contains several petal styles and leaves. Some petals can be used as leaves if cut from green paper. Circles are included in this set, as they make an excellent finishing touch to the back of a blossom.

FLOWER AND FEATHER STICK-ON

Use this feminine spray to embellish a gift box or card front, or wear it as a corsage for an evening. It could even be worn in your hair. The feather boa accent gives it a vintage charm. Begin with a circle as a base. Glue on small sections of a feather boa. Add additional glue to the top of the feathers, let the glue set and build the feature flower. You can add craft stamens to complete the vintage look.

SUPPLIES: Cardstock, tacky glue, miniature feather boa, craft stamens, foam tape

GRAPHIC FILES: Assorted flowers and weeds

MEDALLIONS

Layer flowers and circles with tacky glue and foam tape to make medallions. Use medallions to decorate cards, packages, magnets and tags. Make them large for a stately room décor. Make them in seasonal colors to suit many occasions. How about putting one on a door molding or using it to seal an envelope? Add fishing line and dangle them from the ceiling.

SUPPLIES: Cardstock, tacky glue, foam tape, rhinestone

GRAPHIC FILES: Assorted flowers and circles

Locket

This paper locket is a novelty that can be glued to a blank card, given as a token or used as an interactive element in a scrapbook. A pair of best friends will want to keep identical lockets forever, so make one for each. Celebrate an anniversary and put a photo of you and your loved one inside. You can also use the cutout on the front of the locket for a dimensional element.

MATERIALS & TOOLS

Double-sided cardstock

Paper banner (See page 23 for instructions.)

Tacky glue

Dimensional flower (See pages 64–66 for instructions.)

Half pearl

Ribbon

GRAPHIC FILES

Locket (Cut 2—1 with windows, 1 without.)

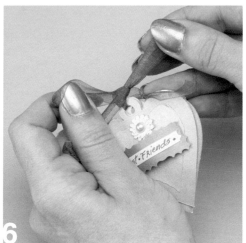

1. Use the hearts left over from cutting out the inside of the frame as a template for the insert, cutting with a 1/8" (3mm) allowance all around so it fits nicely. Glue the hearts to the inside of the windowed locket piece.

2. Glue the locket cover to the back of the locket interior, sandwiching the inserts between and matching up the holes.

3. Fold the locket in half at the hinge to close it. Make sure all the edges line up. Glue the heart you cut out of the frame onto the front as decoration for the locket frame.

4. Glue a banner to the center of the locket front, spanning the heart you just glued on.

5. Glue on a tiny dimensional flower with a half-pearl (see pages 64–66 for instructions) centered toward the top of the locket.

6. Thread ribbon through the locket's top loop and tie a bow.

Mobile

This mobile adds interest and movement to a party or to a child's room. Just a whisper twirls the lightweight line and the paper comes to life. Watch the flowers flutter and the butterflies twirl.

MATERIALS & TOOLS
Double-sided cardstock
Clear glue dots
Tacky glue
Awl
Round nose pliers
Wire cutters or Rosary pliers
Green covered floral wire
Monofilament
Rhinestones

GRAPHIC FILES
Banner Set (BAN 3 and BAN 4)
Butterfly Set (Butterfly 1 [Cut 2 for each desired.], Butterfly Body [Cut 2 for each desired.])
Fox (Cut 2 for each desired.)
Assorted flowers (Cut numerous in varied sizes to build dimensional flowers around wires.)

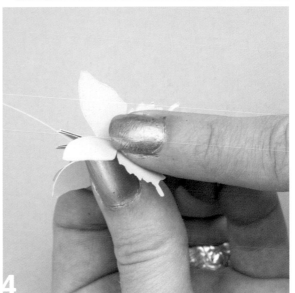

1. Put a dot of glue in the center of your butterfly body. Place some fishing line along the glue line and let it dry completely, making sure that it runs straight through the body.

2. Add another dot of glue and adhere the second butterfly on top. Let it dry completely.

3. Cut the butterfly body in half at the antennae where the fold is. Glue one half of the body to the front of the butterfly and the other to the back. Let the glue dry completely.

4. Put your finger between the front and back wings of the butterfly to open them up. Repeat for the other side.

Tip

Mobiles tangle easily. Wrap each individual wire in tissue paper to keep it separated from the others. Unwrap the mobile carefully and hang it immediately.

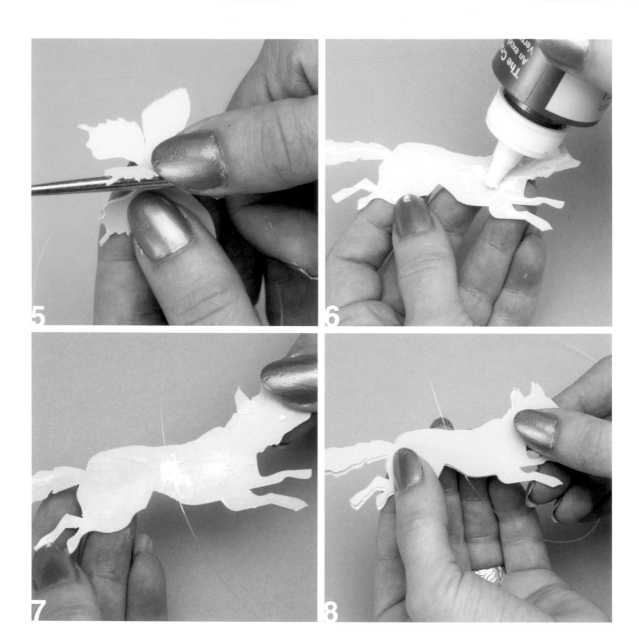

5. Curl the wings using an awl or other round-handled object.

6. Apply glue to one side of the fox, covering the entire area and squeegeeing the glue smooth to the edges with a scrap of paper.

7. Add an extra dot of glue in the middle of the fox's body. Lay the fishing line in the center of the glue.

8. Place the other fox on top, matching it up carefully. Tilt the fox forward on the line to make him run towards the ground, or up to reach for the skies.

9. Before the glue dries, make sure that the fox is centered on the line. You may need to adjust it. Press in the center where the extra glue is, then let the glue dry completely.

10. Put a dot of glue in the center of a green pointed petal flower (this will provide your leaves). Center a piece of fishing line in the glue. Let it dry. Glue another flower to the leaf design.

11. Glue another flower in a contrasting color on top.

12. Finish off with an embellishment. Flip the flower over and build up the flower on the other side in the same way, but without adding another green flower on the other side—the first can act as the leaves for both.

Tip

Embellishments such as acrylic jewels, pearls or stones add a sophisticated accent to projects such as the fox mobile. Many of these accents come with their own adhesives, but you don't always know how strong the bond is, especially with tiny stones. To avoid losing embellishments, dot glue where you want the jewel to go. Remove the protective backing to reveal the jewel's adhesive and press the jewel into place. Allow to dry.

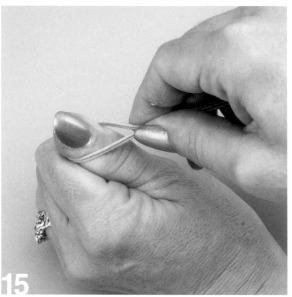

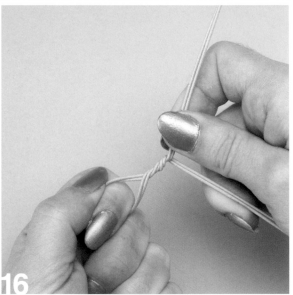

13. To open up the flower, put your fingernail between the green leaves and the flower and push gently. Repeat for all the layers of both sides.

14. Add several elements to each line with 3" to 5" (8cm to 13cm) between elements. To make decorations for the ends of the fishing line, put a dot of glue in the center of the element for the fishing line as with the other decorations, but this time glue the end inside the element.

15. Take the two pieces of floral wire together and bend them in half around your fingers. Pinch the lengths of wire together below your finger to make a loop.

16. Twist the pairs of floral wire around each other three times.

Tip

You can make this project in pieces without the mobile top. Instead of hanging each line on a wire frame, tie a loop at the top of each line and hang the lines separately. Each guest can take one home—what a sweet keepsake of the event!

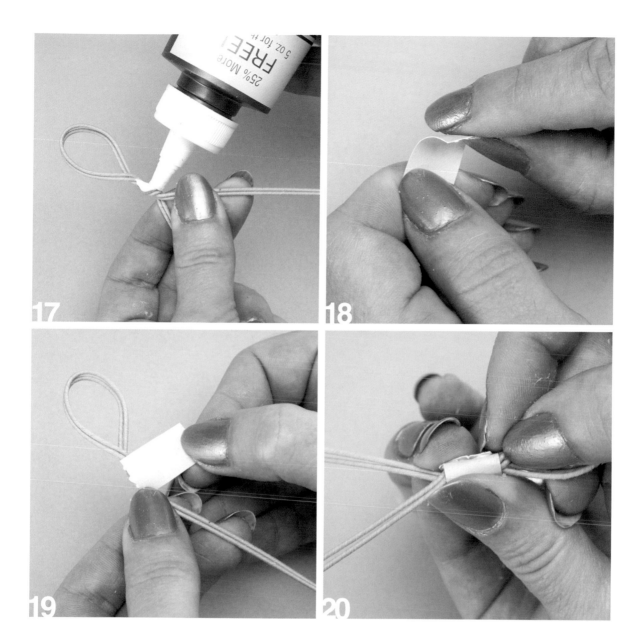

17. Put a dot of glue on the twisted area.

18. Curl your scrap paper a bit to break the grain so that it bends easily and smoothly around the floral wire.

19. Place one short edge of the scrap in the glue dot on the floral wires. Let it dry.

20. Wrap the scrap around the twisted floral wire and glue it in place.

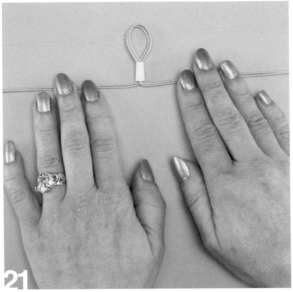
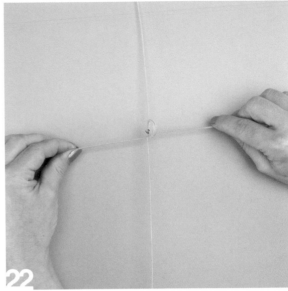

21. Lay your four wire stems out flat on your work surface. Stretch each pair at a 90-degree angle to the loop pointing away from the other pair.

22. Turn the wires so that the loop points up from your work surface. Open up all four arms, creating a large X.

23. With your round nose pliers, make a loop at the end of each wire.

24. Use your hands to bend each arm into a curvy shape. You can use a cylinder (such as a glue bottle) to help you form the curves.

Up for Grabs!

Who gets this gorgeous centerpiece from your party? Write a number on the back of each person's gift tag, inside their place cards or on the back of pieces of coordinating confetti. Draw a number or roll a die to choose the lucky winner.

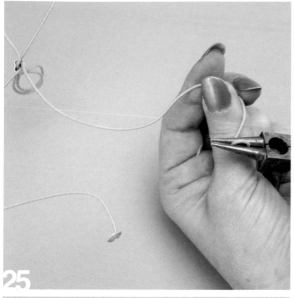

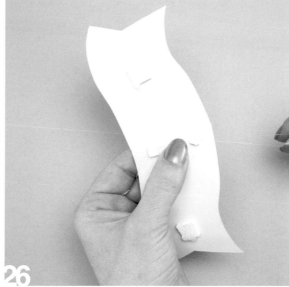

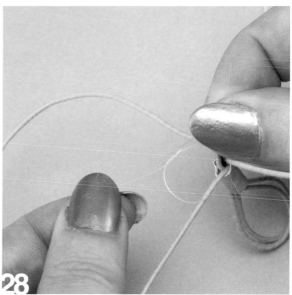

25. With round nose pliers, bend each arm loop down, pointing in the opposite direction from the loop at the top of the assembly.

26. Place a square of foam tape at the center of each end of the back of the larger banner (BAN 3). Place two pieces of foam tape in the center of the banner back. Place fishing line running through the centers of the two foam tape pieces you just placed.

27. Put a drop of glue on top of the fishing line. Match up and adhere the second, smaller banner piece (BAN 4).

28. Tie the banner line around the center of the mobile by going in between two of the arms. Tie one line of embellishments onto each of the four loops at the ends of the arms.

CHAPTER FOUR

Cards

As our world becomes more and more electronic, the more valuable paper seems. A handmade greeting is more touching than an e-mail. Handmade cards—whatever the occasion or sentiment— immediately convey thought and consideration. Make a variety of blank cards in several styles, colors and themes for different tastes and personalities. Have them on hand for any occasion a card is needed. When in doubt, go simple. Or you could have a card party! Provide a wealth of cut designs like shoes, florals and butterflies. Have embellishments, adhesives and blank cards ready to go. Invite friends over for a design frenzy. Estimate that it will take each person an hour per card. Throw a card party as a gift for a friend or split the cost of materials. It's so much fun!

Projects shown: Floral Arrangement Card variation (page 90), Under the Sea Card variation (page 99), Purse Invitation variation (page 80), Simple Leaf Card (page 94), Butterfly Card (page 96)

Purse Invitation

This pearly purse invitation is perfect for a girl party, teen party, shopping excursion, or a birthday card for a purse collector or a clotheshorse. How about using it for thank you notes or a special poem for bridesmaids (created in your wedding colors of course)? The special envelope is designed for hand delivery. Make sure to place it inside a cardboard mailer if you intend to send it by the postal service.

MATERIALS & TOOLS
Double-sided cardstock
Adhesive putty
Clear glue dot
Double-sided tape
Tacky glue
Scissors
Ribbon (about 12" [30cm])

GRAPHIC FILES
Purse Invitation Set (Don't cut PI Closures.)

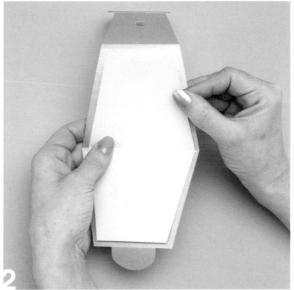

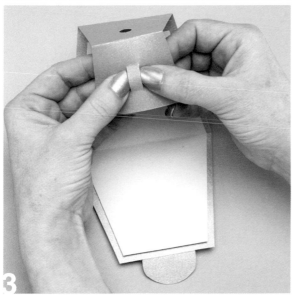

1. Cut out your purse invitation pattern and fold along the lines.

2. Fold the invitation insert piece. Adhere the insert to the inside of the purse invitation with a small clear glue dot, matching up the center folds.

3. Pop both sides of the slot open with your fingernails to create a channel.

4. Cut the ribbon in half. Thread one piece through the channel, making sure it doesn't twist.

Tip

Using a clear glue dot instead of glue on the fold will allow some flexibility of the adhesive so you can open and close the invitation easily.

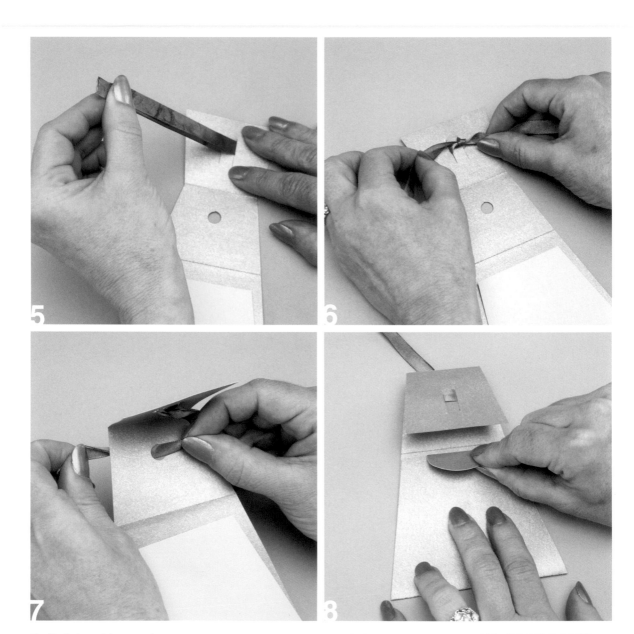

5. Pull the ribbon ends even.

6. Tie a halfknot over the channel. Don't pull too hard or you may damage the paper.

7. Thread both ends of the ribbon through the hole in the flap in the section below the one the channel is in.

8. Fold the bottom of the invitation up to meet the top and bend the semicircle tab down.

Tip

You don't have to throw a party for an excuse to make this project. This is a fun activity for a child (age 8 and up). Make an invitation and allow the child to decorate and trim it. Who knows—you might get invited to the dining room for a pretend tea party like I did!

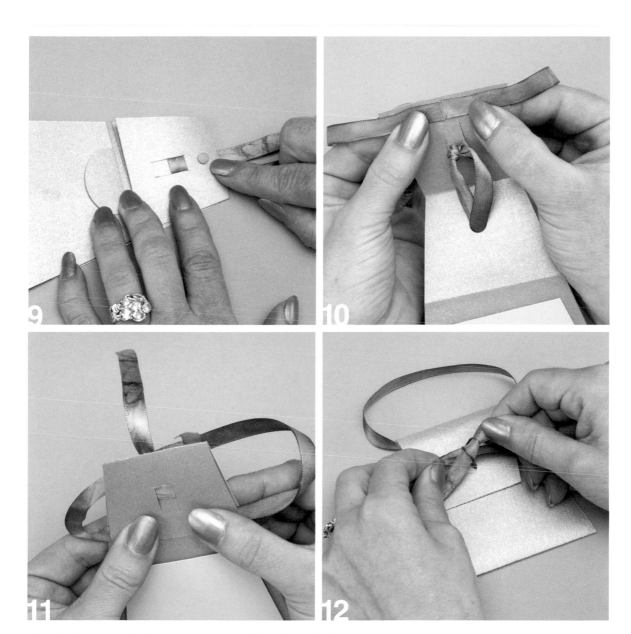

9. Roll a piece of putty into a neat, seed-bead sized ball and press it onto the top of the flap above the channel.

10. Open the top flap again and add a line of glue underneath its top edge. Place the second piece of ribbon with the right side of one end in the glue. Bring the other end around the back of the invitation and place it in the glue as well, making the ribbon into a large loop behind the flap (this becomes the purse handle, as seen in the photo for step 12).

11. Put another line of glue on top of the ribbon ends. Glue the flap down.

12. Fold the purse flap over and tie the front ribbon into a bow. Trim as desired.

Tip

The purse invitation makes a great card for giving a small, flat gift, like cash or a check. Throw in a shopping date and *that's a gift!*.

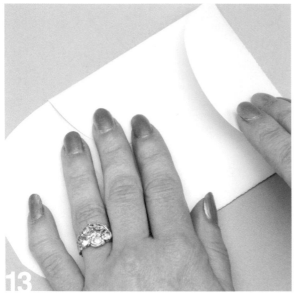

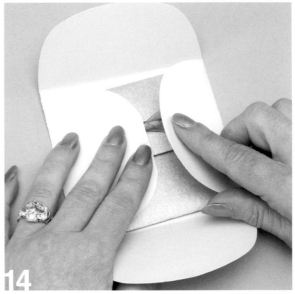

Tip

Since this envelope opens up to lie flat, you can write little messages or words on the insides of the flaps to be viewed together.

Tip

Using putty instead of an adhesive to close the envelope allows it to be resealable. You can also use decorative seals and stickers to close the envelope. Use a lightweight sticker that tears easily. Look for stickers that match or complement your motif and color palette. Gold or silver go with nearly everything.

13. Fold the envelope along the fold lines.

14. Place the invitation inside the envelope and fold the envelope side flaps in.

15. Fold in the top and bottom flaps. Using putty, place a medallion (see page 67) on the flaps to secure them.

Shoe Card

The shoe is a popular, contemporary motif and the pump is timeless. This shoe design makes for a nice all-occasion card or an alternative to the purse invite for a ladies' party. You can use the same envelope for either invitation.

Supplies: Cardstock, patterned paper, tacky glue

Graphic Files: Circles, Purse Invitation Set (PI Envelope, PI Seals), Shoe Set (Shoe 2, Shoe 2 Upper)

Tip

Don't have time to hand make all the invitations? Make an original, scan it, import it into your graphics program and add text. Save and print as many as you need in color. You'll be surprised how well the layered paper look shows up.

Fashion Card

Build up an original paper dress creation on a paper hanger for a fabulous all-occasion card. Your fashion-forward friends will love it and probably have it framed.

Supplies: Cardstock, blank card and envelope, tacky glue

Graphic Files: Hanger, Paper Doll Set (PD Dress 7)

Retro Invitation

This cool invitation will make you want to throw a cocktail party for an excuse to send it! Use this design for a party or a first home or apartment card. Add a guitar and you have a music party. Put a cat on the couch if you are a cat lover. Add metallic accents. Make oversized confetti circles, ovals and pillow shapes for table decor.

MATERIALS & TOOLS

Double-sided cardstock

Tacky glue

Scissors

GRAPHIC FILES

Circles

Retro Set (all Couch and Chair pieces, Lamp)

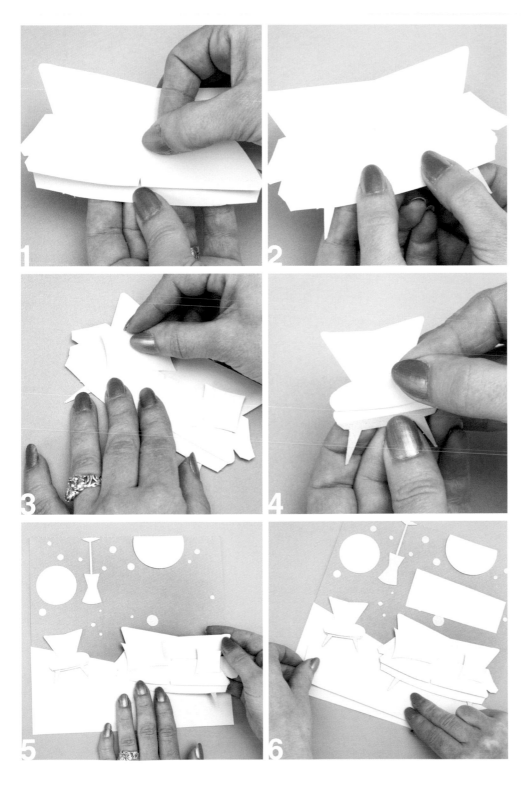

1. Cut the legs off the couch. Adhere the large double seat cushion to the couch.

2. Place glue on the top of the leg trim. Position the leg trim on the back of the couch so the legs show on the bottom.

3. Add the throw pillows.

4. Assemble the chair in the same way, but with the leg trim on the front rather than the back.

5. Add background elements (circles and a lamp) to the background paper, as well as an angled piece of paper for the floor. Arrange your furniture.

6. Place the blanks for the written invitation information.

Fox Invitation

The fox invitation, assembled on a flat (a single panel finished card, like a postcard), uses magnets on the fox and flower note so the recipient can put the small note featuring the important information on the fridge or bulletin board. Your guest won't forget the date of your party, and she'll have a beautiful accent to her kitchen as well.

MATERIALS & TOOLS

Double-sided cardstock

Card flat

Tacky glue

Adhesive putty

Magnet strip

Dimensional flower
(I left mine flat without curling or pinching it.)

GRAPHIC FILES

Fox

Assorted flowers

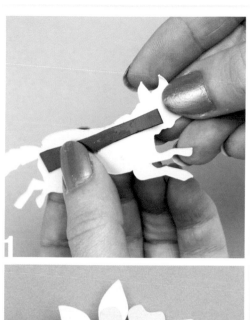

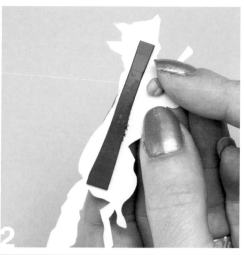

1. Write your announcement on the fox. Cut a piece of magnet to an appropriate size and adhere it to the back of the fox.

2. Put a small piece of putty on the back of the fox underneath the magnet.

3. Glue the flower to a strip of cardstock and write your information on the cardstock.

4. Put a magnet and piece of putty on the back of the flower/card assembly as you did for the fox.

5. Arrange both the fox and flower on the flat.

Floral Arrangement Card

Appropriate for so many occasions, this floral arrangement card in soft greens and white silhouettes pops against the bright background. Cheer up a friend with one or thank a relative or a teacher. Invite a friend to lunch or send a note to say hello.

MATERIALS & TOOLS
Double-sided cardstock
Foam tape
Tacky glue
Scissors
Dimensional flowers
Rhinestone flowers

GRAPHIC FILES
Brambles (Cut several.)
Butterfly Set (Butterfly 1)
Gingko
Seaweed
Trumpet Weeds
Vase Set (Vase 1)

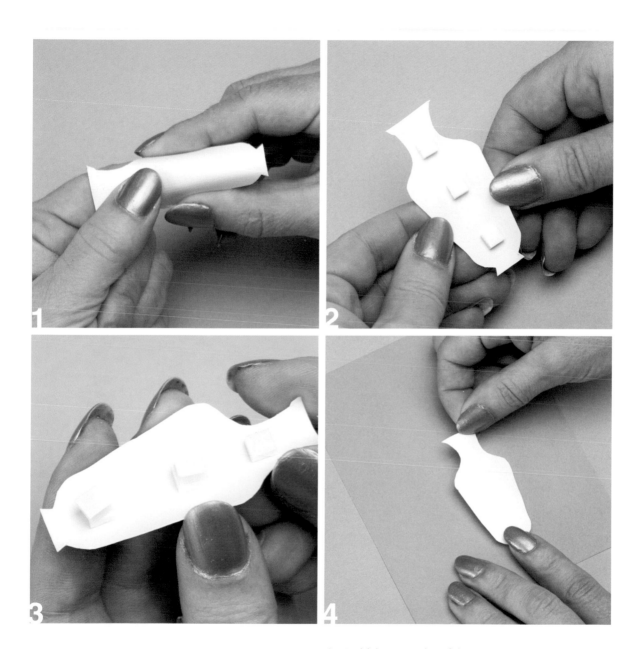

1. Hold the two sides of the vase and bend it lengthwise around your finger.

2. Line three pieces of foam tape down the center of the vase. Put the first piece of foam $1/4$" (6mm) from the top of the vase, leaving room to put stems in.

3. Add another piece of foam tape on top of both the bottom and middle foam pieces.

4. Adhere the vase to the card background.

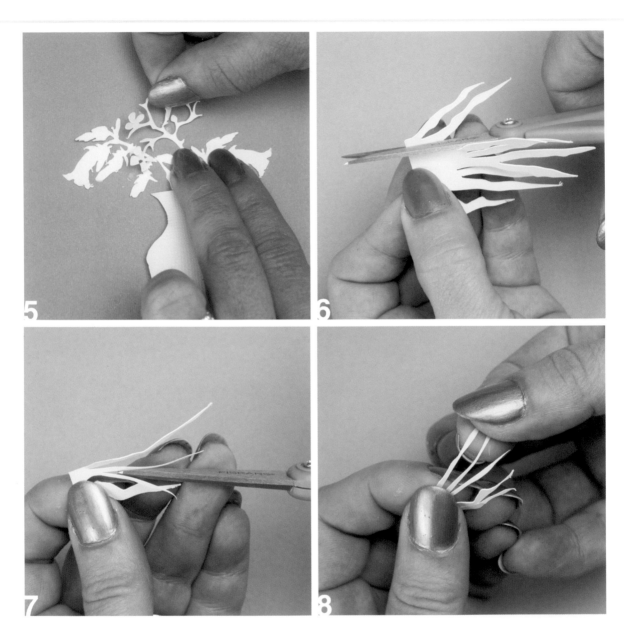

5. Add greenery and filler pieces first by gluing them flat to the background with ends in the mouth of the vase. Work on both sides and then in the middle

6. Cut up the seaweed to make greenery.

7. Make two cuts down the middle of each frond of seaweed, leaving the base intact, to create fine grass.

8. Curl the strands of grass with your fingers, holding the base in place.

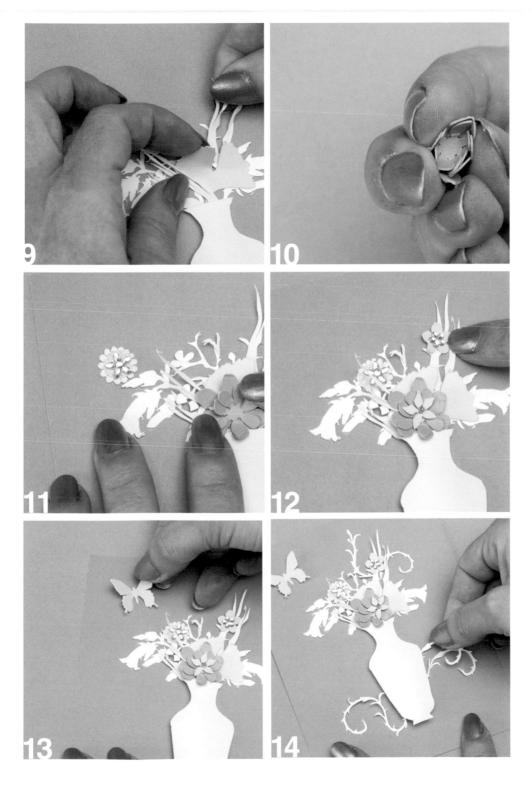

9. Add more dimensional elements, such as a gingko leaf.

10. Crunch a flower between your fingertips to make it dimensional.

11. Glue it onto the card and open it up.

12. Fill in your arrangement with smaller dimensional flowers, some with rhinestone flower centers.

13. Add a complementary element, such as a small butterfly elsewhere on the card.

14. Finish the arrangement with a flourish of brambles. Notice how several pieces of the same design (brambles) repeated in different places add rhythm to the overall composition.

SIMPLE LEAF CARD

For what occasion would this simple motif not be appropriate? Cut the simple leaf detail out of the interior of a leaf or layer it on top for oodles of combinations. Use scraps to hand cut blocks of color or use geometrics such as an oval as the base for your design. Use foam tape or glue to adhere the leaf cuts onto the blocks, using glue sparingly. Glue or tape the design block onto a card flat.

SUPPLIES: Cardstock, decorative paper, vellum, card flats, decorative-edged scissors, scissors

GRAPHIC FILES: Simple Leaf Set

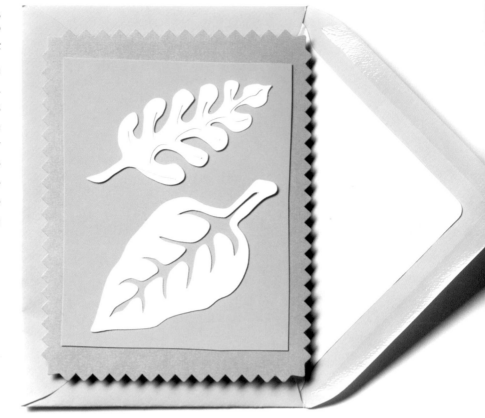

Tip

Always plan ahead with vellum so the glue or tape is covered with a design element and does not show.

Tip

Card flats can be made into postcardlike, two-sided cards or mounted onto blank greeting cards.

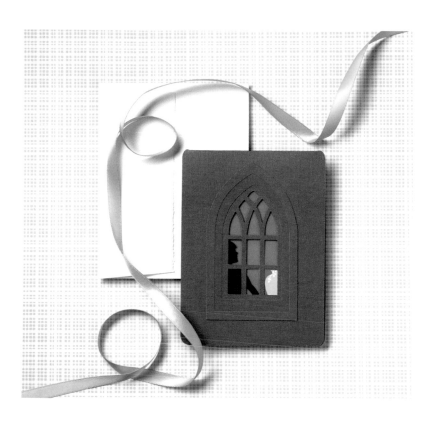

WINDOW SCENE CARD

An arched window, similar to the one featured in the *Arched Window Lantern* (page 107), is the focus of this charming card. Textured cardstock enhances the architectural quality of the layered design. The vellum adds interest and surprise. Use the thinnest window frame from the set as a template and cut the vellum by hand. Place design elements between the inside of the window and the vellum before adhering it. Finish the inside of the card with a rectangle of vellum cut by hand with decorative scissors. Place a battery-operated tea light inside and the card will light up like a lantern.

SUPPLIES: Cardstock, vellum, tacky glue, scissors

GRAPHIC FILES: Arch Window Card Set, Mermaid, Vase Set (Vase 3)

FLOWER BURST CARD

A flat, detailed spray of paper flowers is designed much like a corsage. It seems to burst with joy and thoughtfulness. The frayed ribbon adds textural interest to the arrangement. Make and give this card as a bouquet that lasts forever. Begin with a scrap or circle of paper to use as a base to construct the spray. Build your arrangement on top of the ribbon, leaves first, finishing with one large flower. Notice the green pearl leaves are made dimensional and the other leaves are flat.

SUPPLIES: Cardstock, blank greeting card, tacky glue, acrylic gems, ribbon

GRAPHIC FILES: Circle, assorted flowers and leaves

Butterfly Card

This card, done in bright papers, will bring cheer to someone you care for. The butterfly is simply embellished with chalk ink and rhinestones. It is a sweet example of combining motifs—the butterfly and the flower. Both are curled or crimped to give a little life to the composition. Give this card as a flat (shown) or mount the flat onto another blank card. Handmade cards should be hand delivered or hand cancelled at the post office (not put through a postal machine).

MATERIALS & TOOLS
Double-sided cardstock
Card flat
Tacky glue
Chalk ink pads
Rhinestones
Dimensional flower

GRAPHIC FILES
Brambles
Butterfly Set (Butterfly 1 and Butterfly Body)
Leaf Set (L1 and L6)

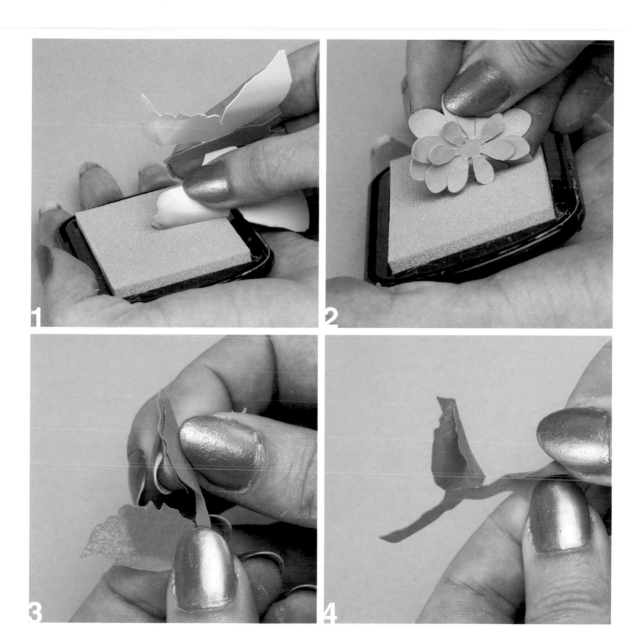

1. Construct a butterfly (see steps 1–4 on page 39 for instructions). Holding your butterfly at an angle between your forefinger and thumb, carefully sweep color from the ink pad onto the edge ⅓ of each wing.

2. Construct a dimensional flower (see steps 1–7 on pages 65–66 for instructions). Sweep chalk onto the entire flower. Holds its front toward the ink pad, swiping ⅓ of the surface at a time.

3. Crimp the ends of all the leaves. Pinch the individual leaves in half.

4. On the bigger leaves, fold back one edge of each leaf, giving it a curly wave.

5. Glue some rhinestone accents on the tips of each wing.

6. Add a dot of glue on the lower right-hand corner of the card front. Add your greenery, placing the tips of the stems in the glue and splaying the leaves out from there.

7. Glue on your dimensional flower, placing its center over the tips of the leaf stems. Add a rhinestone to the flower's center.

8. Add the butterfly. Put the brambles on last to even out the design. Put glue only on the ends of the brambles that go under the flower, leaving the other ends free to meander.

CUPID CARD

Appropriate for any loving occasion, cupid is an ancient motif. The cupid design makes a bold graphic statement, so it is easy to make a quick card with some real punch. Stack circle cuts on top of one another for a background. Glue or tape Cupid to the center of the background. Finally, adhere the assembly to the front of a blank card and you're finished! These cards are a snap. Make a bunch. Spread the love.

SUPPLIES: Cardstock, decorative papers, blank card with envelope, double-sided tape, tacky glue, decorative scissors

GRAPHIC FILES: Angel, Circle

UNDER THE SEA CARD

A peek into a deep world, these underwater scenes seem almost animated. Pearl, glitter and metallic papers shift the light, creating visual movement. Bright colors bounce, seaweed seems to wave, layers of translucent vellum make soft, floating jellyfish. A little foam tape behind fish and rocks furthers the dimensional effect. Hand cut the blue glitter background imperfectly, continuing a fun, animated style.

SUPPLIES: Double-sided cardstock, foam tape, tacky glue, scissors

GRAPHIC FILES: Coral Set (Coral 2, Rocks), Fish Set (Fish 2), Jellyfish, Kelp, Seaweed, Starfish

CHAPTER FIVE

Lanterns

Paper lanterns make a great gift for anyone, especially the hard-to-buy-for. Make earthy lanterns for those with simple tastes using minimal or no themed decorations. Make lanterns magical with layers of decorative mattes and three-dimensional elements, like trees or cord. Imagine a secret forest, a pearly seascape or a quiet ridge of fir trees. The soft flicker of a battery-operated LED tea light is as soothing a light as a real candle, without the risk of fire—these lanterns are not meant for use with real candles. Eliminating an open flame means you can place lanterns where you couldn't before: in a playroom, under framed artwork, against a wall—you decide! No smoke. No fire.

Paper lanterns make dreamy nightlights, especially in a guest room or a dark hallway, and these handmade treasures bring a warm touch of home to campers, cabins and RVs. Imagine them hanging on branches during a still night or ornamenting guests' plates at a bridal dinner. With all the design sets included, you are limited only by your imagination.

Projects shown: Hanging Vellum Lantern variation (page 108), Screen Lantern variation (page 111), Arched Window Lantern variation (page 107)

Bamboo Kitty Cottage Lantern

Set a dimensional scene inside this little cottage lantern. The set comes with miniature mats that frame the motif you choose. This lantern shows off a bamboo-kitty combo. Layer design elements on the inside of the vellum for a theatrical shadow effect.

MATERIALS & TOOLS
Double-sided cardstock

Tacky glue

Foam tape

Awl

Battery-operated tea light

GRAPHIC FILES
Bamboo

Cat 2

Cottage Lantern Set (CL Mattes 1 and 2, CL Roof and Cottage Lantern [Cut 2—do not cut the smaller of the two windows.])*

Assorted leaves and weeds

* For a tea light to fit properly in the lantern, the lantern files must be cut at actual size.

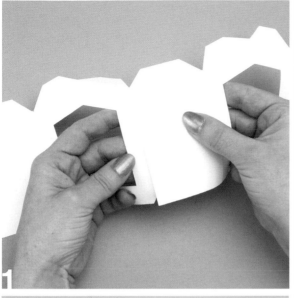

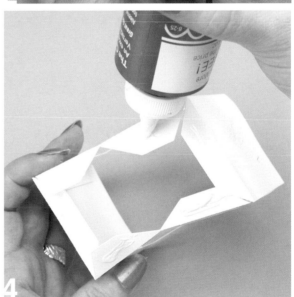

1. Put glue on the side tab of one of the lantern sides and glue the edge of the smaller part of the second side piece to it, matching up the corners.

2. Fold along the fold lines to create a box. Glue the second set of side flaps together.

3. Fold the top flaps down and in toward the center of the box.

4. Apply glue to the center of each top tab and spread evenly over them.

Tip

Did you know you can get battery operated LED tealights and votives made of real wax? Some are scented to add another dimension to the experience. Consider investing in rechargeable tea lights or candles if you love to be enchanted by light as I do. LED bulbs last a long, long time.

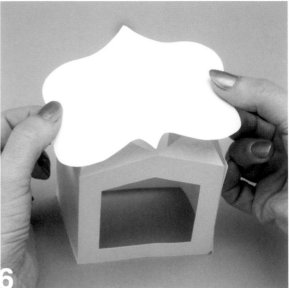

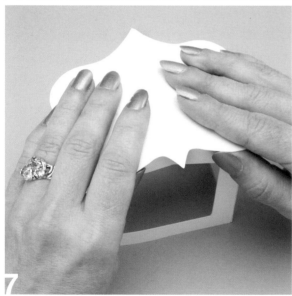

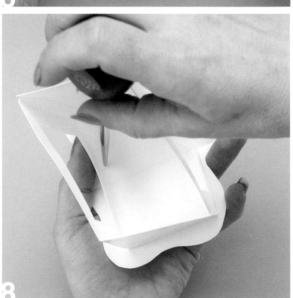

5. When the glue on the tabs forms a skin, it is ready. Push the tabs upward a bit so they easily catch the roof. Make sure the lantern sides are squared off and even so the roof sits flat.

6. Place the folded roof on top of the flaps. Match the point of the roof up with the points in the centers of the larger sides.

7. Apply light pressure to the top to adhere the roof. Use your fingers to make sure the tabs are in contact with the roof.

8. If you have trouble, push down on the tabs from inside the lantern with an awl to make sure there's good contact.

Tip

For an animated effect, place two lights in one lantern. Try a combination of a candle-flicker and a color-changing tea light.

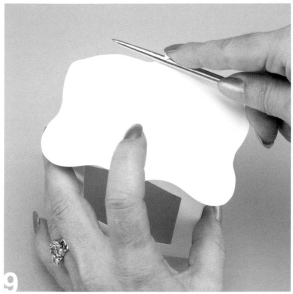

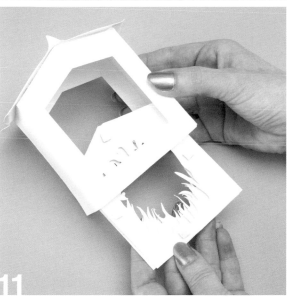

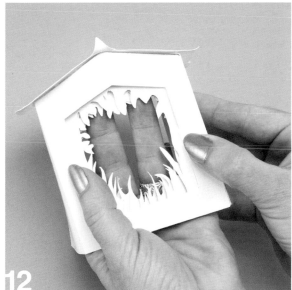

9. Use an awl to curl up the edges and peak of the roof. Work carefully to avoid making rigid crease lines.

10. Layer three different frame mattes with foam tape between the layers at the top, bottom and sides of the pieces.

11. Add another layer of foam tape onto the front of the top matte. Remove the protective covering from the foam tape and slide the mattes into place inside one of the lantern windows. Take care to avoid the exposed adhesive making contact before the mattes are completely in place.

12. Put light pressure on the back of the matte stack to help adhere it to the inside of the cottage window.

Tip

Add a pinch of adhesive putty to the bottom of a lantern to help hold it in place on a table or shelf.

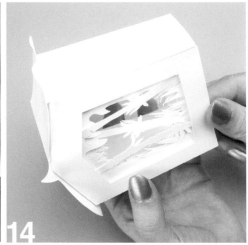

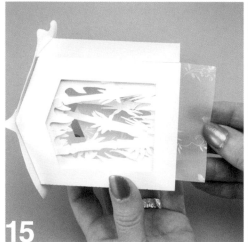

13. Slip design elements in between the frame and the mattes and attach with dots of glue. Put the glue on the front side of the elements.

14. Get as detailed as you like, putting elements in each layer.

15. Cut a piece of vellum slightly larger than the lantern window to fit inside. Apply small dots of glue at the edges on the front of the vellum. Slide the vellum into place and hold for a moment to adhere to the lantern matte.

16. Add the final design element, in this case a cat, gluing it right on the front edge of the frame.

Note

All tea lights are not equal. Look for the number of hours on the package. Some claim 150 hours. Many seasonal tea lights are not meant to last.

Tip

You can make tiny holes in a vellum window with a sewing needle for a twinkle effect.

ARCHED WINDOW LANTERN

Arched windows have a classic appeal. Simple motifs work best for this lantern because of the elegant crisscrossing of the panes. The window trim completes the architectural look. You can choose to cut the arch without the panes, an especially good option if cutting by hand.

SUPPLIES: Cardstock, vellum, tacky glue

GRAPHIC FILES: Arch Lantern Set*

* For a tea light to fit properly in the lantern, the lantern files must be cut at actual size.

GUEST OF HONOR LANTERN PLACE CARD

There won't be any question of where the guest of honor sits at your party. Dim the lights in the dining room and the flickering, battery-operated tea light inside this lantern place card will light the way to a great time. What a precious gift for your dear one.

SUPPLIES: Cardstock, vellum, tacky glue, permanent fine-tip pen

GRAPHIC FILES: Brambles, Cottage Lantern Set (CL Roof and Cottage Lantern)*, Fir Line

* For a tea light to fit properly in the lantern, the lantern files must be cut at actual size.

Hanging Vellum Lantern

This hanging lantern folds into a box with two windows. I chose a simple leaf pattern to fill the large window. This design includes a paper bezel for the window and a decorative reinforcement for the hanger. The side gusset adds interest to the shape. The example shown can also be used as a gift box with or without the windows

MATERIALS & TOOLS
Double-sided cardstock
Vellum
Tacky glue
Organza ribbon
Battery-operated tea light

GRAPHIC FILES
Ferns (Cut several.)
Gusset Box Lantern Set*

For a tea light to fit properly in the lantern, the lantern files must be cut at actual size.

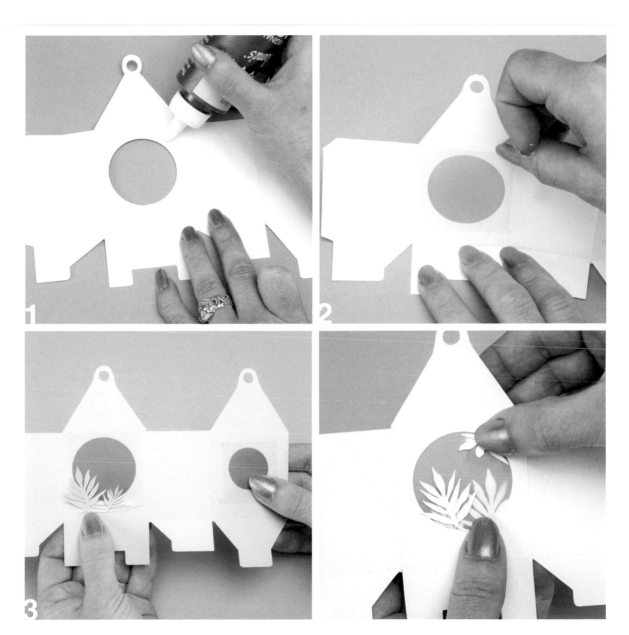

1. On the back side of the lantern, put dots of glue ¼" (6mm) apart around the circle window cutout.

2. Cut a square of vellum a little larger than the window. Lay the vellum in place on the glue dots.

3. Arrange some design elements on the back side of the vellum window. Adhere using a generous amount of glue outside the circle of the window (you don't want the glue to show up through the vellum).

4. Turn the lantern over and continue to compose the design. Adhere new elements within the circle of the window on the front of the lantern.

5. Carefully glue the circle frame to the circle window, finishing off the scene. Make sure that the ends of elements don't poke out beyond the frame. If they do, carefully trim them off.

6. Take the eyelet embellishment and glue it to the top of the lantern, matching up the holes. Repeat for the other eyelet on the other side of the lantern.

7. Assemble the box, gluing the tabs in place and pinching in the gussets.

8. Tie a bow through the eyelets at the top of the lantern and carefully insert a battery-operated tea light, making sure it doesn't catch on the design elements as you lower it in.

HANGING CONE LANTERN

Made to hold a tea light when hung upside down, this lantern is small but unique. Single motifs, such as a leaf, a flower or a star look best in this little window. Decorative mini clips make opening and closing the top of the lantern to turn the tea light on and off easier. These would be pretty hanging from branches placed in a vase as a centerpiece.

SUPPLIES: Cardstock, vellum, tacky glue, mini decorative metal clip

GRAPHIC FILES: Triangle Lantern Set*, assorted decorative motifs

* For a tea light to fit properly in the lantern, the lantern files must be cut at actual size.

SCREEN LANTERN

This design reminds me of an old fashioned folding screen. It offers a generous design area and can be made with one window or four. Adhere design elements to the inside of the vellum for a shadow effect or on the outside for a splash of color.

SUPPLIES: Cardstock, vellum, tacky glue

GRAPHIC FILES: Brambles, Screen Lantern*, Seahorse

* For a tea light to fit properly in the lantern, the lantern files must be cut at actual size.

Conclusion

The silhouette is a timeless expression, a familiar and lasting art form that began when a caveman blew pigment through a reed, leaving an outline of his hand. We immediately understand this simple representation by its outline. Silhouettes can be as simple as one tree on a contrasting background or as sophisticated as a lantern with a grove of trees and a curious deer. I hope the projects and designs I have created for you encourage you to make your own paper art gifts, keepsakes and charming accents for your home and life's special events. Explore all of the designs on the CD (you can get a quick glimpse of the whole array in the index to cutting designs that follows). Mix and match, alter and embellish to your heart's desire. The projects in this book are just the beginning!

Index to Cutting Designs on CD-ROM

These thumbnails represent the gallery of .eps and .pdf design files on the included CD. Refer to page 17 of the *Materials and Techniques* section or the Read Me file on the CD for more information on importing them into the correct format for your computer or cutting machine.

Design Key

RED LINES: DETAIL AND INTERIOR CUTTING—CUT FIRST.
(SOME RED LINES ARE OPTIONAL, SUCH AS A WINDOW ON A BOX OR LANTERN.)
BLUE LINES: FOLD (POUNCE) LINES—CUT (PERFORATE) SECOND.
BLACK LINES: SILHOUETTE OR OUTSIDE CUT LINES.

Gusset Box Lantern Set

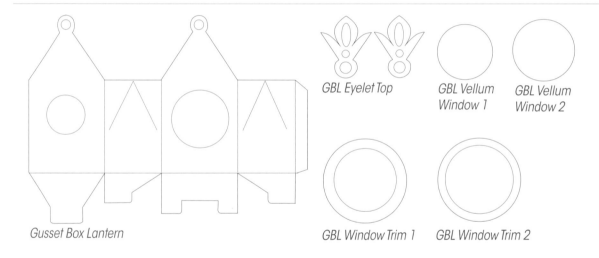

Gusset Box Lantern

GBL Eyelet Top

GBL Vellum Window 1

GBL Vellum Window 2

GBL Window Trim 1

GBL Window Trim 2

Forest Matte Set

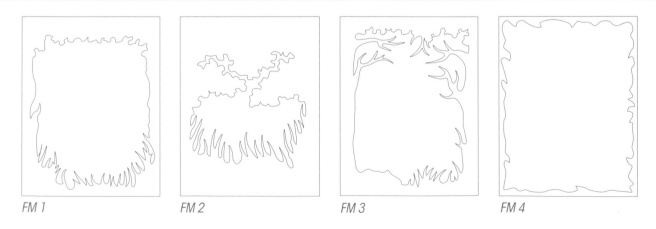

FM 1

FM 2

FM 3

FM 4

Arch Lantern Set

Arch Lantern

AL Trim 1

AL Trim 2

Triangle Lantern Set

Triangle Lantern

TL Trim 1

TL Trim 2

Arch Window Card Set

Arch Window Card

AWC Trim 1

AWC Trim 2

AWC Trim 3

Cottage Lantern Set

Cottage Lantern

CL Matte 1

CL Matte 2

CL Matte 3

CL Roof

Mini Lantern Set

Mini Lantern

ML Trim

ML Vellum Window

Screen Lantern

Simple Lantern

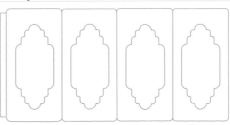

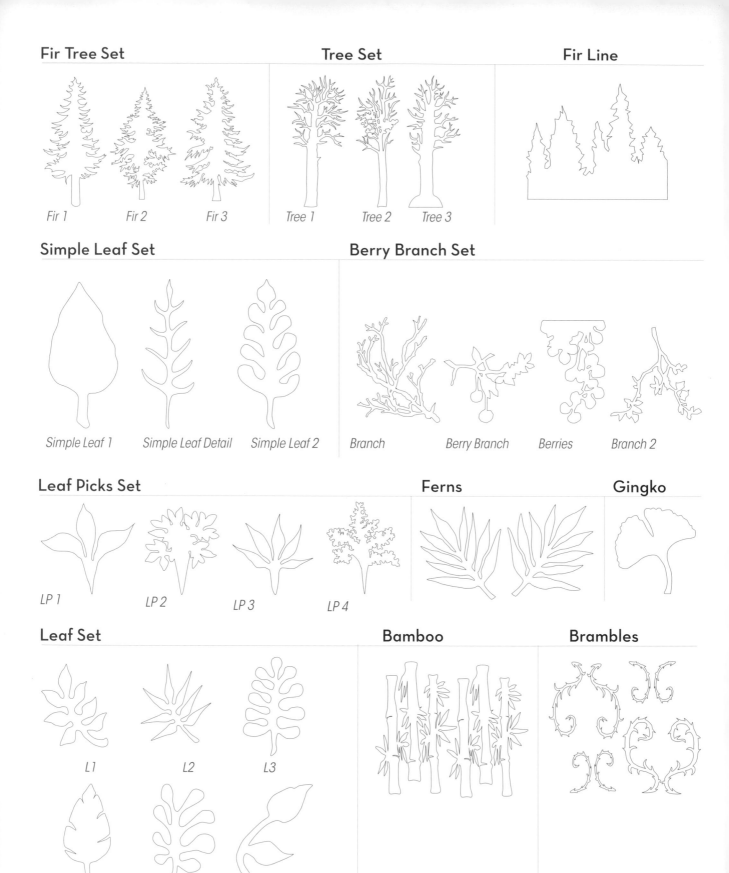

Fir Tree Set

Fir 1   *Fir 2*   *Fir 3*

Tree Set

Tree 1   *Tree 2*   *Tree 3*

Fir Line

Simple Leaf Set

Simple Leaf 1   *Simple Leaf Detail*   *Simple Leaf 2*

Berry Branch Set

Branch   *Berry Branch*   *Berries*   *Branch 2*

Leaf Picks Set

LP 1   *LP 2*   *LP 3*   *LP 4*

Ferns

Gingko

Leaf Set

L1   *L2*   *L3*

L4   *L5*   *L6*

Bamboo

Brambles

116

Flower Set A

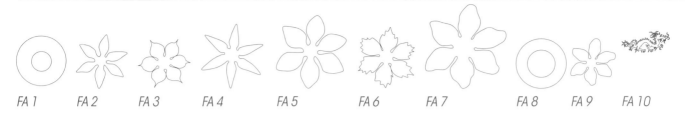

FA 1   FA 2   FA 3   FA 4   FA 5   FA 6   FA 7   FA 8   FA 9   FA 10

Flower Set B

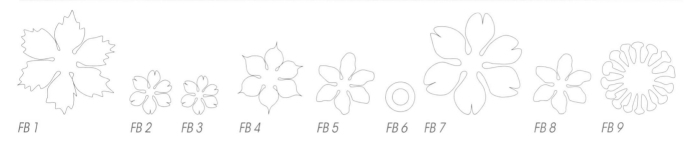

FB 1   FB 2   FB 3   FB 4   FB 5   FB 6   FB 7   FB 8   FB 9

Flower Set C   Weeds

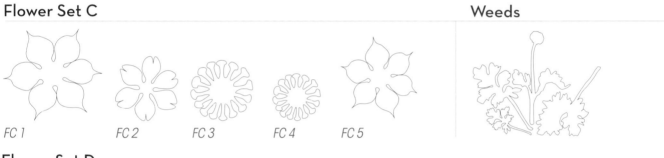

FC 1   FC 2   FC 3   FC 4   FC 5

Flower Set D

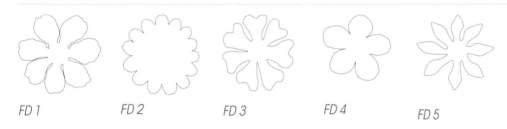

FD 1   FD 2   FD 3   FD 4   FD 5

Star Flower   Mod Flower   Cherry Blossom Set

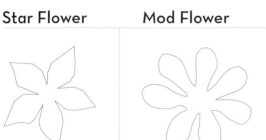

Cherry Blossom   *Cherry Blossom Details*

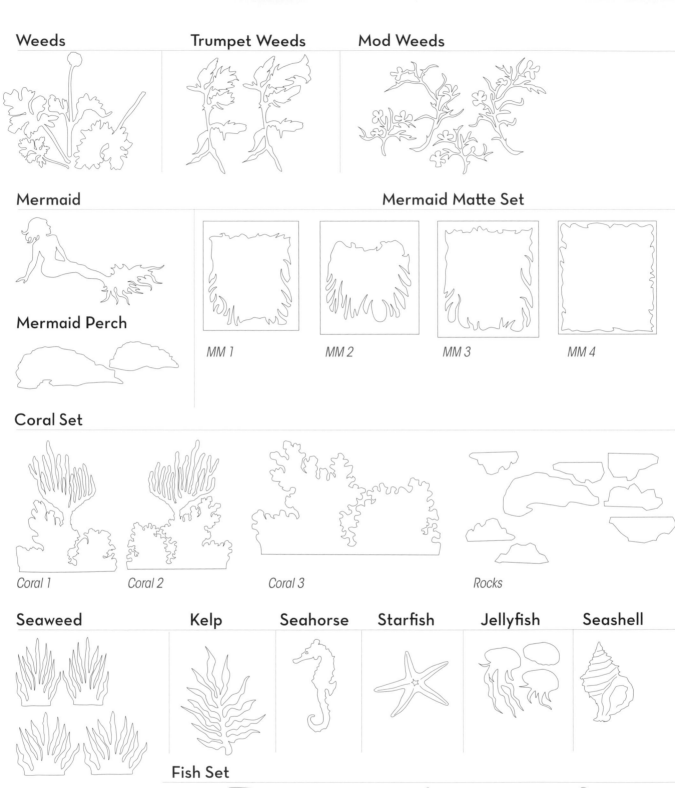

Weeds

Trumpet Weeds

Mod Weeds

Mermaid

Mermaid Matte Set

MM 1

MM 2

MM 3

MM 4

Mermaid Perch

Coral Set

Coral 1

Coral 2

Coral 3

Rocks

Seaweed

Kelp

Seahorse

Starfish

Jellyfish

Seashell

Fish Set

Fish 1

Fish 2

Fish 3

Moon and Stars Set

Moon and Stars

Moon Background

Wolf Set

Wolf Front   *Wolf Back*

Butterfly Set

Butterfly 1   *Butterfly 2*   *Butterfly Body*

Cat 1   ## Cat 2

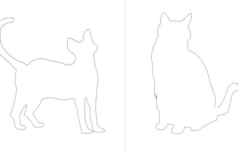

Dragonfly Set

Dragonfly Wings   *Dragonfly Body with Legs*   *Dragonfly Body*

Deer Set

Deer Front   *Hinge*   *Deer Back*

Bird Set

Bird 1   *Bird 2*   *Bird 3*

Fox

Rabbit

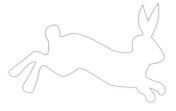

Dragon

Guitar Set

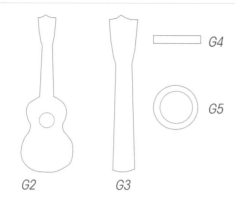

G1   *G2*   *G3*

G4

G5

Bridge

Geisha Garden Set

Geisha   *GG Lantern*   *GG Bamboo*   *GG Green 1*   *GG Green 2*   *GG Flowers*   *GG Green Set*

Castle Set

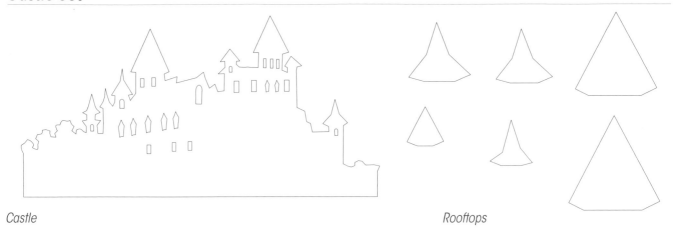

Castle

Rooftops

Castle Green Set

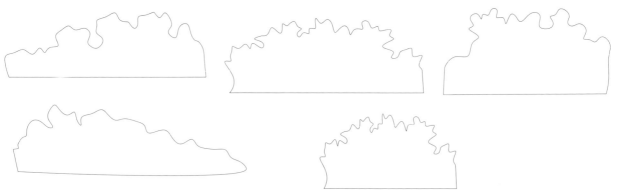

Doll Ornament Set

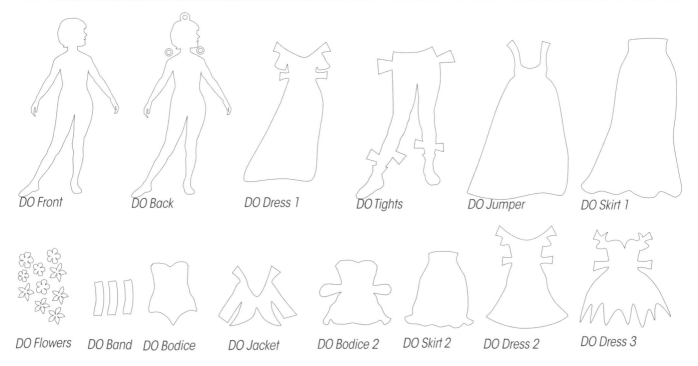

DO Front

DO Back

DO Dress 1

DO Tights

DO Jumper

DO Skirt 1

DO Flowers

DO Band

DO Bodice

DO Jacket

DO Bodice 2

DO Skirt 2

DO Dress 2

DO Dress 3

Paper Doll Set

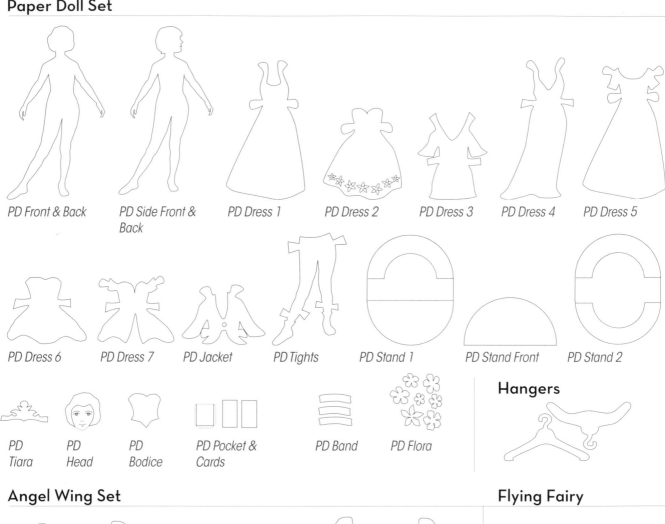

PD Front & Back

PD Side Front & Back

PD Dress 1

PD Dress 2

PD Dress 3

PD Dress 4

PD Dress 5

PD Dress 6

PD Dress 7

PD Jacket

PD Tights

PD Stand 1

PD Stand Front

PD Stand 2

PD Tiara

PD Head

PD Bodice

PD Pocket & Cards

PD Band

PD Flora

Hangers

Angel Wing Set

Wing 1

Wing 2

Wing 3

Flying Fairy

Shoe Set

Shoe 1

Shoe 1 Upper

Shoe 2

Shoe 2 Upper

Shoe Trim

Fairy Wings

Angel

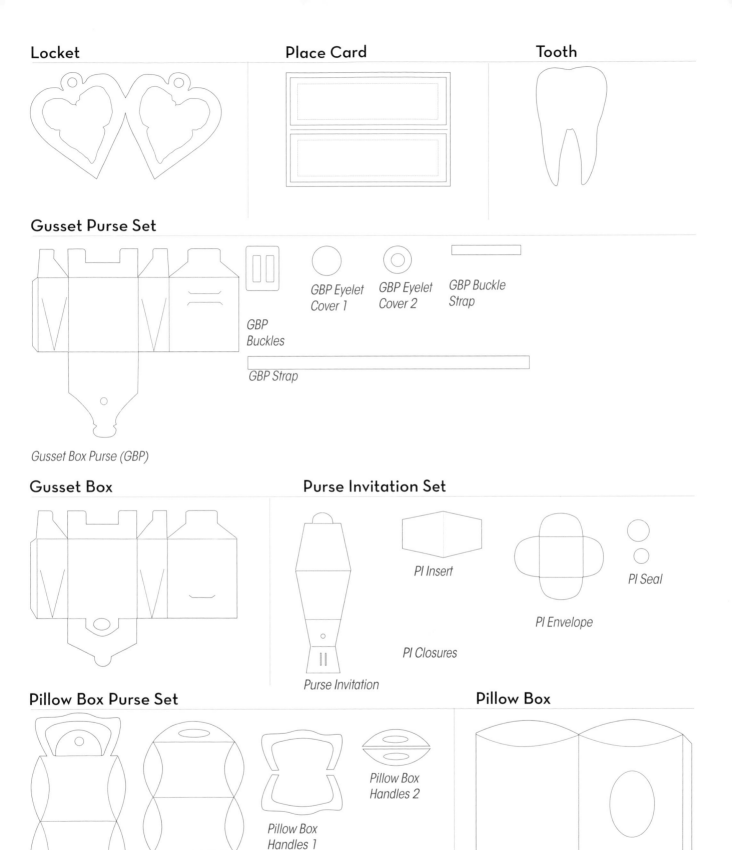

Locket

Place Card

Tooth

Gusset Purse Set

GBP Buckles

GBP Eyelet Cover 1

GBP Eyelet Cover 2

GBP Buckle Strap

GBP Strap

Gusset Box Purse (GBP)

Gusset Box

Purse Invitation Set

PI Insert

PI Seal

PI Envelope

PI Closures

Purse Invitation

Pillow Box Purse Set

Pillow Box

Pillow Box Handles 1

Pillow Box Handles 2

Pillow Box Purse 1

Pillow Box Purse 2

Banner Set

BAN 1   BAN 2   BAN 3   BAN 4

Buckle Set

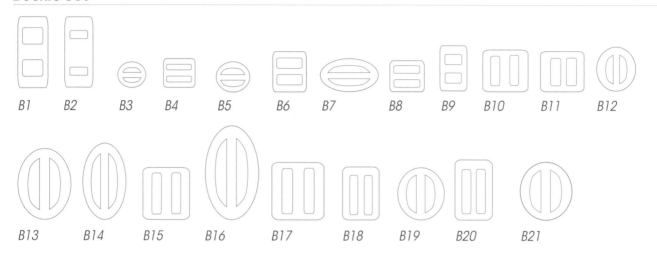

B1   B2   B3   B4   B5   B6   B7   B8   B9   B10   B11   B12

B13   B14   B15   B16   B17   B18   B19   B20   B21

Tag Set

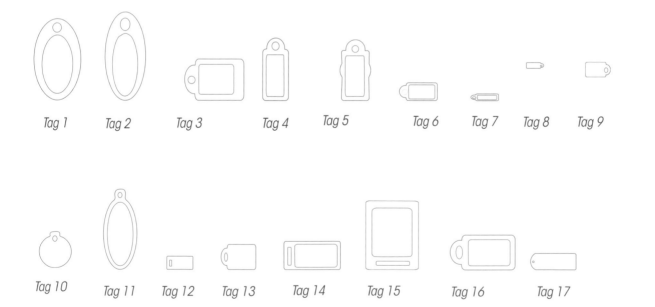

Tag 1   Tag 2   Tag 3   Tag 4   Tag 5   Tag 6   Tag 7   Tag 8   Tag 9

Tag 10   Tag 11   Tag 12   Tag 13   Tag 14   Tag 15   Tag 16   Tag 17

Retro Set

Couch

Couch Cushion

Couch Frame

Couch Pillows

Lamp

Chair

Chair Cushion

Pillows

Chair Frame

Frame

Rug

Sunburst

Coffee Table

Centerpiece

Martini Glass

Vase Set

Vase 1

Vase 2

Vase 3

Vase 4

Vase 5

Vase 6

Circle

Resources

**Accugraphic, Inc.,
or KNK USA**
*Klik-N-Kut MAXX, Blades,
Paper, Vinyl, Tech Support*
(800) 268-3672
www.accugraphic.com/
www.scrapbookdiecutter.com

Duncan Enterprises
*Assorted craft supplies,
paints, adhesives*
5673 East Shields Ave.
Fresno, CA 93727
(559) 291-4444
www.duncancrafts.com

EK Success Ltd.
Paper Crafts and Tools
100 Delawanna Avenue
Clifton, NJ 07014
(973) 458-0092
www.eksuccess.com

Fiskars
*Scissors, Shape Cutters,
Wavy-Edged Scissors*
www.Fiskars.com

Gaunt Industries, Inc.
Aleene's Tacky Glue
9828 Franklin Avenue
Franklin Park, IL 60131
(847) 671-0776
www.aleenestackyglue.com

**Martha Stewart Living
Omnimedia, Inc. or Martha
Stewart Create**
*Glitter, Paper, Glue, Flocking,
Microbeads, Cutting Tools,
Punches*
www.marthastewart.com/crafts

Provo Craft
Terrifically Tacky Tape
151 East 3450 North
Spanish Fork, Utah 84660
(800) 937-7686
www.provocraft.com

Tracey Packaging, Inc.
Stencil/Oil Board
112 Leo Avenue
P.O. Box 647
Syracuse, NY 13206
(800) 639-5664
www.traceypackaging.com

Index

Indulge your creative side
with one of our other fine titles...

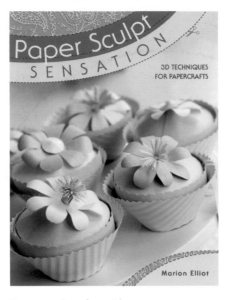

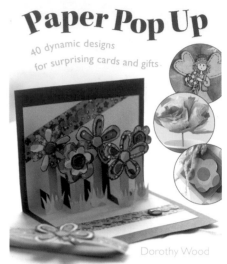

Delight in the Details

by Lisa M. Pace

Delight in the details of papercrafting! Lisa Pace will inspire you with more than 40 techniques for creating embellishments that provide a finishing touch to any papercraft project. Hand stitches, shimmering wire sprays and crepe paper rosettes are just some of the techniques you'll learn to make your creations extra-special. Try your hand at 100 delightful projects—from greeting cards, to scrapbook layouts, to home décor. Plus, peak inside the author's studio where pretty vintage details come to life. Delight in the Details helps you make every detail count!

paperback; 8.25" × 10.875"; 128 pages
ISBN-10: 1-59963-085-0
ISBN-13: 978-1-59963-085-4
SRN: Z3054

Paper Sculpt Sensation

by Marion Elliot

Discover the diversity of three-dimensional designs that can be created with paper in this step-by-step guide to paper sculpting. You'll be able to master the basics, which include folding, bending, curling, pleating and stitching in order to transform paper into sensational creations. A wealth of inspiring project ideas feature crafting favorites, such as intricate frames, gift boxes, paper "desserts" and even jewelry. A bonus gallery of variation ideas provides added inspiration.

paperback; 8.25" × 10.75"; 128 pages
ISBN-10: 0-7153-2973-1
ISBN-13: 978-0-7153-2973-3
SRN: Z3685

Paper Pop Up

by Dorothy Wood

Surprise and delight friends and family with hand-crafted pop-up cards and gifts guaranteed to bring a smile. Learn to craft 40 dynamic pop-up designs from cards, to a colorful interactive advent calendar, to board books and a fun Easter gift box. Incorporate elements like pull tabs, slider bars, turning wheels, envelope reveals and stunning pop-ups. Inspirational mixes of paper, embellishments and fabulous colors, plus easy-to-follow step-by-step techniques, ensure results that really rise to the occasion!

paperback; 8.5" × 11"; 112 pages
ISBN-10: 0-7153-2430-6
ISBN-13: 978-0-7153-2430-1
SRN: Z0904